ARMSCOR

SOUTH AFRICA'S ARMS MERCHANT

ARMSCOR

SOUTH AFRICA'S ARMS MERCHANT

by

JAMES P. McWILLIAMS

BRASSEY'S (UK)

(A member of the Maxwell Pergamon Publishing Corporation plc)

LONDON · OXFORD · WASHINGTON · NEW YORK

BEIJING · FRANKFURT · SÃO PAULO · SYDNEY · TOKYO · TORONTO

UK	Brassey's (UK) Ltd.,
(Editorial)	24 Gray's Inn Road, London WC1X 8HR, England
(Orders)	Brassey's (UK) Ltd.,
	Headington Hill Hall, Oxford OX3 0BW, England
USA	Brassey's (US) Inc.,
(Editorial)	8000 Westpark Drive, Fourth Floor, McLean,
	Virginia 22102, USA.
(Orders)	Pergamon Press, Inc., Maxwell House, Fairview
	Park, Elmsford, New York 10523, USA.
PEOPLE'S REPUBLIC	Pergamon Press, Room 4037, Qianmen Hotel,
OF CHINA	Beijing, People's Republic of China
FEDERAL REPUBLIC	Pergamon Press GmbH, Hammerweg 6, D-6242
OF GERMANY	Kronberg, Federal Republic of Germany
BRAZIL	Pergamon Editora Ltda, Rua Eça de Queiros, 346,
	CEP 04011, Paraiso, São Paulo, Brazil
AUSTRALIA	Brassey's Australia Pty Ltd., P.O. Box 544, Potts
	Point, NSW. 2011, Australia
JAPAN	Pergamon Press, 5th Floor, Matsuoka Central
	Building, 1-7-1 Nishishinjuku, Shinjuku-ku,
	Tokyo 160, Japan
CANADA	Pergamon Press Canada Ltd., Suite No. 271, 253
	College Street, Toronto, Ontario, Canada M5T 1R5

Copyright © 1989 Brassey's (UK) Ltd.

First edition 1989

Library of Congress Cataloging in Publication Data
McWilliams, James P.
Armscor: South Africa's arms merchant /
James P. McWilliams.
1st ed.
p. cm.
Bibliography: p.
1. Armaments Corporation of South Africa Ltd.
2. Munitions—South Africa.   I. Title.
UF537.A44M38   1989   355.8'2'0968—dc20
89-33880

British Library Cataloguing in Publication Data
McWilliams, James P.
Armscor: South Africa's arms merchant.
1. South Africa. Military equipment. Weapons.
Acquisition. International political aspects
I. Title
355.8'2'0968

ISBN 0-08-036709-7

Printed in Great Britain by BPCC Wheatons Ltd, Exeter

Contents

Preface

Armscor*: South Africa's Arms Merchant has developed through an intense interest in Africa in general and Southern Africa in particular.

My hunger for knowledge of the politico-military-economic nuances of this vast continent was nurtured by the dedicated and astute academicians at Howard University, Washington, D.C., particularly those in the African Studies and Research Programme. Africa means many things to many people but once you have landed on its soil, you acquire an affinity that is difficult to explain to those who have not done so. To me, Southern Africa is one of the most beautiful yet complex areas on the face of the globe. One never tires of the flora and fauna, the fascination of its many races or the delight of its superb climate.

Perhaps, one day all will be in the spirit of harmony that, unhappily, is absent today. I have indeed been fortunate to have been able to see some of the best and some of the worst of Southern Africa. The more that I see and absorb, the more I realise the scale of the area's problems and appreciate what the various political groups are trying to achieve. I can offer no instant answers to these problems, like so many of the 'five day junket' visitors to the area. Like Mao Tse Tung, I too believe that empirical knowledge comes first from the experience of doing. I still have an overwhelming array of questions to resolve, many ideas and little time for casting stones or making hasty judgements. The complexity of it all does not lend itself to 'hip pocket' analysis. Nobody is completely informed, nevertheless, the gullibility of the uninformed is frightening.

The fact that I received no grants or any monies from any organisation in support of my research and travels permitted me to write about the scene as I saw it. There are no hidden obligations to anyone. The research, views and analysis are mine, based on many

---

*Armaments Corporation of South Africa Limited.

months of reading, observing, travelling, interviewing and talking to numerous people of various political persuasions.

By design, the reader is given a wide appreciation of the role of Armscor in the politics and economy of South Africa and, hopefully, a better understanding of 'South Africa's Arms Merchant'. Statesmen and academics will find more food-for-thought on the South African question. Finally politico-military analysts interested in Southern Africa are presented with a stepping stone for additional in-depth analysis.

Reams of technical data on weapons systems were systematically reviewed by the author but not included in this book. It was essential to study all this data to ensure that the specific capabilities of various weapons systems did actually exist and that they were not the imagination of the Public Relations Department of Armscor. To overload the reader with it would have been counterproductive. As an aside, I requested, but was not granted, permission for a briefing by Armscor. Their reasoning was, 'You are not sponsored by any of our sponsoring agencies.' Of course I wasn't, for I preferred to be no one's client. I also spent some time in the Union Buildings, Pretoria. Unfortunately, a meeting with a Director of Foreign Affairs, at which I requested ready access to various ministries and military officials for interviews on Pretoria's defence posture, led to another refusal. Although emphatically stating my case as an objective researcher, recent statements by the United States Secretary of State, George Shultz, and President Reagan had evidently upset the Foreign Ministry and, as I was an American, they were not very open with me although a 12-month research visa was granted by the South African Embassy in Washington.

To my knowledge there is no one book that deals completely with Armscor. Whether this is because of a lack of public interest or the official veil of secrecy over information on the subject, one cannot be certain. Nevertheless, it is my profound hope that the reader will be given a more comprehensive understanding of the role of Armscor within the South African system of government and of the impact of the Armaments Corporation of South Africa Limited on the South African Defence Force and the international Arms market.

Acknowledgements

I would like to extend my gratitude to the many people who, throughout my travels in Southern Africa, afforded me the opportunity to gain much insight into the politico-military-economic situation in the region.

I wish to express my thanks and appreciation to Professor Robert Edgar for his invaluable guidance throughout my research and studies at Howard University, Washington, D.C. His open-mindedness and willingness to listen to all sides on the complex issues of Southern Africa were refreshing. He always provided different dimensions to contemporary events in the region. In short, he demands of himself and others the necessity of logical and analytical thinking.

I would be remiss if I did not acknowledge the many dedicated and astute academicians at Howard University, particularly those in the African Studies and Research Programme, who nurtured my hunger for knowledge of this vast, complex region.

A special thanks goes to Professor John Barratt and the staff at the South African Institute of International Affairs located at Witwatersrand University in Johannesburg. I utilised the research facilities at SAIIA extensively. The staff were most helpful and went out of their way to help me.

There were many people to whom I spoke on an informal and formal basis. Unfortunately, they are too numerous to mention but my full gratitude goes out to them. These included politicians, academics, Armscor personnel, military officers, business men and women, police officers and South Africans, both black and white. I had no formal briefings by Armscor but they did, however, provide an array of weapon system photographs that were used in my research and some of which are reproduced in the text. My catalogue of these photos has been invaluable and I would be remiss if I did not thank those responsible for providing them.

I am indebted to Maureen Demot, lecturer, author and my

professional contact in South Africa. She has assisted me by opening doors that otherwise would have been closed to a foreigner. A well done goes to Lulu Samawi and Anne Slonin for their untiring aid throughout the process of typing and editing many drafts.

Finally, and most importantly, I must acknowledge my six pillars of support who have always encouraged me to 'go for it' – my wife, Jane; my three sons, J.P., Mark, and Derek and my daughters, Coleen and Deirdre. No man is an island nor should he ever have to be.

List of Plates

Glossary of Abbreviations

ANC	African National Congress
Armscor	Armaments Corporation of South Africa Limited
BBC	British Broadcasting Corporation
BLS	Botswana, Lesotho, and Swaziland
BOSS	Former South African Centralised Intelligence Agency
CCSA	Christian Concern for Southern Africa
COSATU	Congress of South African Trade Unions
CSIR	Council for Scientific and Industrial Research
D-RI	Democrat – Rhode Island
DSAA	Defence Special Account Act
DTA	Democratic Turnhalle Alliance
ECCM	Electronically Controlled Counter Measures
FAPLA	People's Armed Forces for the Liberation of Angola
G5	155 mm Howitzer
G6	155 mm Howitzer, self-propelled
GNP	Gross National Product
GRINEL	Grinaker Electronics (Pty) Ltd.
HWD	Howaldtswere – Deutsche Werft
IDC	Interdepartmental Committees
IKL	Ingenierkontor Luebeck
IISS	International Institute for Strategic Studies

JMC	Joint Management Centre
LAVI	Israeli Fighter Aircraft Project. Lavi is a Hebrew word, meaning 'son of a lion'.
LEW	Lyttleton Engineering Works
MPLA	Popular Movement for the Liberation of Angola
NATO	North Atlantic Treaty Organisation
NIDR	National Institute for Defence Research
NSMS	National Security Management System
PAC	Pan African Congress
PACS	Political Action Committees
PMP	Pretoria Metal Pressings
R	Rand
R&D	Research and Development
RPV	Remotely Piloted Vehicle
RSA	Republic of South Africa
SA	South Africa
SAAF	South African Air Force
SABC	South African Broadcast Corporation
SADCC	Southern African Development Coordination Conference
SADF	South African Defence Force
SAIIA	South African Institute of International Affairs
SAN	South African Navy
SAS	South African Ship
SATS	South African Transport Services
SCR	Security Council Resolution
SSC	State Security Council
SWA	South-West Africa (Namibia)
SWANU	South-West African National Union

SWAPO	South-West African People's Organisation
SWAPO-DM	South-West African People's Organisation – Democrats
TM57	Anti-tank Mine (Soviet)
UDF	United Democratic Front
UNITA	National Union for the Total Independence of Angola
UNTAG	United Nations Transitional Administrative Group
XHI	Experimental Helicopter ONE

1

Why Armscor?

If one looks at the South African Defence Force (SADF), it becomes apparent that it is the strongest defence force in Africa in terms of trained manpower, organisation, weapons systems, mobilisation capacity and defence budget. The Republic of South Africa has the capability to procure and manufacture the overwhelming majority of its weapons and armaments through its existing agency, Armaments Corporation of South Africa Ltd. (Armscor).

According to *The Military Balance, 1988–89,* published by the

PLATE 1.1   Eland 60 Armoured Car

1

International Institute for Strategic Studies (IISS), South Africa has 250 Centurian/Olifant tanks, 1,600 Eland armoured cars, 1,500 Ratel infantry combat vehicles, 324 combat aircraft, 14 armed helicopters and 134 other helicopters. The SADF can mobilise 558,500 personnel of whom 455,000 are in the Reserves. Defence expenditures for 1985/86 were 2.27 billion dollars. The defence budget for 1986/87 indicated allocations of 2.012 billion dollars. The 1987/88 budget sought commitment authority of R6,903 million for defence, an increase of 29.7 per cent or R1,580 million (approximately $790 million).

This year's (1988/89) budget is R8,196 million (approximately $4.097 billion).[1]* The defence budget states that the R8 billion represents 15.2 per cent of total state expenditure for 1988/89, or 4.2 per cent of South Africa's gross domestic product.

According to the Minister of Defence, General Magnus Malan, South Africa is 95 per cent self sufficient in military production. In initiating its 'preparedness programme' long before the 1977 mandatory arms embargo by the West, General Malan said that the Republic was self-sufficient. This term embraces the conception, design and development of armaments less the 5 per cent needed from the outside for tools and technical assistance.[2] Speaking at the unveiling of the newest addition to South Africa's defence arsenal, the Cheetah fighter aircraft, in 1986, President P.W. Botha underscored the importance of technologically superior weapons systems when he said:

> It is known that there has been a continuous build-up of weapons on our borders during recent years. It is therefore logical that we anticipate the threat and prepare ourselves accordingly. For this reason we have come to expect that Armscor and the Defence Force ensure our security and we expect them to be at the forefront of technology.[3]

Mr. Botha reiterated his theme song that South Africa has developed its own highly sophisticated arms industry since the arms embargo against the Republic. He emphasised that the Armaments Corporation of South Africa had already achieved success in foreign marketing and 'forcing the world to take cognisance of the unique ability which exists in South Africa...'[4] Corroborating Botha's statement is the Report of the United States Secretary of State's Advisory Committee on South Africa which states:

> The South African Defence Force occupies an important position in the country's power structure ... is the best trained and equipped

---

*See Appendix A.

military on the African continent. It is widely believed that the South African government possesses the ability to develop a tactical nuclear weapon capability. [The report goes on] The military's political influence and direct participation in the highest councils of government have increased substantially...[5]

The Arms Embargoes

The question of the arms embargo against South Africa has intensified the debate over whether, because of the embargo, South Africa is now less dependent on outside sources, having established a degree of independence in armament manufacture not hitherto achieved. Some pundits have argued that the arms embargo has not produced the result that the international community intended but rather has managed to create a stronger SADF, less dependent on the political whims of arms sales from external sources. The Secretary of State's report seems to follow this logic.

In response to an international arms embargo begun on a voluntary basis in 1963 and made mandatory by the UN Security Council in 1977, South Africa has also developed its own independent arms industry, Armscor, the state-owned armaments corporation, is now the

PLATE 1.2   Armscor Laboratory

third largest industrial group in the country, with some 16,000 employees. By 1985, South Africa's arms industry was ranked as the tenth largest in the world, and reportedly fulfilled roughly 85 per cent of the country's requirements. It is generally agreed that this would not have been possible without direct or indirect assistance from foreign sources (notably Israel, France and Taiwan). The recent announcement that South Africa has built its first prototype jet fighter (the 'Cheetah') is illustrative of this point.[6]

With the foregoing in mind, the role of Armscor becomes of critical importance. Therefore, the problem to be investigated is the role of Armscor in the military, political and economic structure of the Republic of South Africa (RSA). This empirical study on the role of Armscor establishes the interlocking industrial corporate structures that support Armscor. Links with other national states and/or bodies are established as a corollary.

Armscor's objective is to meet the Republic of South Africa's diverse armament needs. In terms of its mandate, it must do so in an efficient and economical manner, and by the maximum utilisation of the local industries of the private sector.

An examination of the United Nations arms embargo as a spur to armaments production in South Africa will be pursued. The principal contents of the compulsory United Nations Security Council resolution passed on the 4th of November 1977 reads:

> The Security Council, acting therefore under Chapter VII of the Charter of the United Nations.
> 1. DETERMINES, having regard to the policies and acts of the South Africa Government, that the acquisition by South Africa of arms and related material constitutes a threat to the maintenance of international peace and security.
> 2. DECIDES that all states shall cease forthwith any provision to South Africa of arms and related material of all types, including the sale or transfer of weapons and ammunition, military vehicles and equipment, paramilitary police equipment, and spare parts for the aforementioned and shall cease as well the provision of all types of equipment and supplies and grants of licensing arrangements, for the manufacture or maintenance of the aforementioned.
> 3. CALLS on all states to review, having regard to the objectives of this resolution, all existing contractual arrangements with the licenses granted to South Africa relating to the manufacture and maintenance of arms, ammunition and vehicles, with a view to terminating them.[7]

Domestic Arms Production

Since the Second World War, there has been armament production in South Africa. An Advisory Committee on Union Defence Equipment Requirements was appointed in October 1948 to investigate and report on the Union's industrial potential for warlike equipment. In 1949 the Committee became the Defence Resources Board, which existed until 1966.

Lyttleton Engineering Works, which was previously the Defence Ordnance Workshop, was established in 1953 by the Defence Production Office. Its directive was to provide a stockpile of technical information and manufacturing techniques, and to supply munition requirements. It was replaced by the Armaments Production Board, established during 1964 in terms of the Armaments Act, Act No. 87 of 1964. 'During 1968, the Armaments Development and Production Corporation was established with the sole purpose of taking over and managing the two existing factories of the Armaments Production Board and certain strategic facilities owned by private industry.'[8] In referring to the establishment of Armscor, the Corporation's own glossy brochure *This is Armscor*, states:

> During April 1977, the Armaments Production Board and the old Armscor amalgamated with a view to controlling the procurement and

PLATE 1.3 Lyttleton Engineering Works

production of all armaments by one organisation. In this way the Armaments Corporation of South Africa Ltd. came into being. Armscor's subsidiaries are at present manufacturing a wide range of strategic products varying from aircraft to small-arms ammunition. Private sector industries are requested to produce items ranging from combat vehicles to warships and electronic equipment, and they are also responsible for supplying components and subassemblies....[9]

Armscor generates interest as an integral part of the larger dimension of the South African question. As such, the role of the Corporation becomes critical in the execution of the policies of the South African Government. If South Africa is able to counter the mandatory arms embargo through circumventing it and/or satisfactorily manufacturing its armaments needs, the so-called embargo becomes mute.

As the world's major gold producer, South Africa's economy has been able to expand significantly into other industrial areas, forming a solid national economic base and so reducing its vulnerability to foreign pressures. With this in mind, the Republic's armaments industry becomes increasingly important. It follows, then, that the scope, direction and role of Armscor, coupled with the domestic industry's interlocking structures, are important facets in meeting the needs of the country's future security. Therein lies the interest in this subject – the economic power, political will, public determination, technical expertise and zeal of the Republic, coupled with its pariah status in the international community happen to be a unique subject that warrants study.

Although various sorts of pressure are being exerted on South Africa, there is little visible evidence that the Republic is meaningfully modifying its policy on political franchise. Indeed, as we have seen, a matter of concern is the possibility that sanctions and the arms embargo may have the opposite effect. This study seeks to show a cause/effect relationship, albeit not comprehensively, of the arms embargo and the growing self-sufficiency of the South African Defence Industry. It shows too that the broad scope of Armscor's programmes and the defence policy, as outlined in the latest South African *White Paper on Defence and Armaments Supply*, are indicators of the Republic's determination to resist any pressure leading to a meaningful rapid change on racial policy.

New Responsibilities for Armscor

The decolonisation of Angola and Mozambique generated concern in South Africa about the possibility of a conventional threat from these potentially hostile governments. In the wake of these events, the Republic moved to strengthen its self-sufficiency in selected areas particularly in armaments. In doing so, private industry was put on notice that it would be tasked to provide strategic items in the interest of defending the country from the threat. The central repository for weapons systems procurement and acquisition was placed on the doorstep of Armscor. Within this mandate Armscor assumed the responsibility covering the entire process of weapons production from research through development and manufucture to servicing, parts and repair/overhaul.

Coincidentally, other events acted as catalysts in Armscor's creation in response to the RSA's increased security and defence requirements. International criticism, domestic turbulence in the black communities, the insurgency in Namibia, sanctions and the arms embargo hastened the necessity for a monolithic co-ordinating body for the domestic control of weapons systems. Thus, the result was the rising prominence of Armscor with the attendant industrial, political and economic power. Commandant Piet Marais, Chairman of Armscor, speaking on the number of people employed in armaments production emphasised that Armscor was 'the third or fourth biggest employer in South Africa'.[10]

According to Kenneth W. Grundy, 'Frankel sees this as a "lower order version" of C. Wright Mills' concept of the military-industrial complex. The analogy is not inappropriate … Armscor exists solely to improve the material defence capabilities of the state.'[11] Grundy goes on in an attempt to give a clearer picture of Armscor in terms of a military-industrial complex.

> It may be a bit overdrawn to speak of a military-industrial complex in Millsian terms. The American model is so deeply entrenched and so much larger and more elaborate. But the 'partnership', as Deon Geldenhuys calls it, is genuine and mutually supportive. Many firms now have vested interests in seeing their links with the Defence Department flourish and in the process they may help to influence government decisions on armament questions as government has been able to influence the firms. On logistical matters the interaction is undeniable. Whether it extends to larger strategic questions is doubtful. If Armscor should begin to develop an export capacity, then business input into foreign decisions might expand.[12]

It should be noted contrary to Grundy's assertion 'if Armscor should begin to develop an export capacity', that Armscor has developed an export capacity.[13]

2

The United Nations Arms Embargo and the Creation of a South African Arms Industry

Background to the 1963 United Nations Voluntary Arms Embargo

As all the world knows *apartheid* is South Africa's highly controversial economic, political, and social system based on race. It is buttressed by a complex legal structure and security apparatus that tends to channel wealth, power, and privilege in the hands of the white minority. Historically and systematically, *apartheid* began before its proclamation in 1948. Its roots have been and are embedded in the issue of land. The bantustans (homelands) and the tightly regulated supply of labour, coupled with the basic thread of *apartheid* ideology emphasising cultural difference, are examples of *apartheid's* controversial nature. With the 1948 electoral victory of the Nationalists, *apartheid*, as an ideology, evolved and was implemented in an elaborate system of laws. The ideology is manifested in a single principle – the complete separation of the races.

After 1948, but particularly after the assumption of the prime ministership by Verwoerd in 1958, government domestic policy was directed toward this end. By the creation of separate states for blacks out of the old native reserves, the white elite hoped to eliminate Africans from the South African heartland with the intention of creating 'foreigners' in search of temporary employment.

From 1948 onwards, political trends in the non-Western world generally, and sub-Saharan Africa in particular, were such as to make the political demography of South Africa increasingly foreboding. This postwar situation posed a dilemma for the Afrikaner leadership. How could they suppress the emerging black political and economic power and at the same time gain international legitimacy? *Apartheid* was essentially the Afrikaner's solution to this problem.

The Verwoerdian plan of separate development became the core of *apartheid* strategy after 1960 – the creation of ethnic homelands, the requirement that blacks become citizens of homelands and eliminating genuine black political expression. Obviously, the system of *apartheid* failed, despite South Africa's attempts to make it internationally palatable.

South African Response to External Pressures

In 1948, deep-seated Afrikaner nationalism reflected a growing opposition to South Africa's traditional close ties with Britain. Consideration was given to developing strong defence forces whilst, at the same time, freeing the Republic from the dependence on Britain. This thinking was the direct result of the reopening of the ammunition plants under the Defence Resources Board which had been inactive since the Second World War. Generally speaking, defence procurement tended to come from Britain until South Africa left the Commonwealth in 1961. After that time procurement from France was dominant with the exception of cooperative construction of naval patrol boats from Israel.

The relatively low level of weapons production during the mid 1940s and 1950s gave way to Pretoria's development of greater military self-sufficiency in light of two major setbacks in 1960 – violent black unrest erupted throughout the country and the Republic was pressured to leave the Commonwealth.

After the confrontation between black protesters and police at Sharpeville on 21 March 1960, in which the police were panicked into opening fire, killing 69 people and wounding 180, Pretoria's defence expenditure was geared chiefly to the suppression of internal unrest and the intimidation of potential insurgency movements. That incident also gave a significant boost to international action to bring about the end of *apartheid*, a mood that intensified in an atmosphere of rapid de-colonisation which influenced much of the rest of the African continent.

The 'winds of change' were gathering momentum and South Africa needed strong military forces in order, eventually, to dominate the southern African region. In addition, a militarily strong South Africa could defy the United Nations over issues pertaining to the region, particularly South West Africa (Namibia). Added impetus to the growth of militarisation was South Africa's penchant for passing itself off as a valuable military ally of the West. Thus, in order to fulfil its goals, large amounts of money were spent on armaments and defence.

The Sharpeville incident acted as a catalyst to the outside world for the public boycott campaign focusing on pressuring governments for an arms embargo against South Africa. Traditional arms suppliers came under fire from internal public opinion and Afro-Asian countries. In March 1963, the newly elected Labour party leader of Great Britain, Harold Wilson, was strongly in favour of a boycott. In August of that year, the United Nations Security Council called on all states to cease the sale and shipment of armaments to South Africa. In this same month, the United States decided to support the United Nations embargo. South African defence expenditures were R44 million in 1960–61, increasing 61 per cent in 1961–62, 293 per cent in 1962–63, and continuing to increase to 579 per cent in 1966–67 to R255 million.

In April 1963, Defence Minister Andre Fouche stated that his government had all the weapons it needed to maintain internal order.[1] On 27 October 1963, Professor Le Roux of the Council for Scientific and Industrial Research announced that a new National Institute for Rocket Research would be established near Pretoria to develop a ground-to-air missile. In the same year, Defence Minister Fouche requested monies for research in rocketry. Internal arms production was made a priority based on the response of the international arms embargo. Newspaper reports made reference to poison gases such as Tabun, Soman, and Sarin being developed in South Africa. Although not substantiated, these colourless, odourless and tasteless gases added considerable fuel to the fire in the United Nations debates on an international arms embargo against South Africa.

Furthermore, by 1965, the Republic had already obtained 120 licences to manufacture weapons locally and was practically self-sufficient in the production of small weapons and small calibre ammunition. Preparations for building aircraft started in 1965, and in 1967, Atlas Aircraft Corporation began producing Italian Impala jet aircraft under licence. A large number of the technicians were previously dismissed aircraft workers from Britain. Also, in 1965, a new naval base was under construction which would be an addition to Simonstown. Close cooperation with Britain was maintained. During March 1968, the Chairman of a British ship building firm which had previously built three of South Africa's frigates, was on record as saying he would expand his interests in South Africa to include building warships. In May 1968, Defence Minister, P.W. Botha, introduced the Armaments Amendment Bill. The object of the new legislation was to create the Armaments Development and Production Corporation of South Africa – Armscor.

South Africa continued to build its armament stockpile during the 1960s. Napalm bombs, anti-armour mines, night sights and the undertaking to build locally the first naval vessel and the establishment of a missile base on the Zululand coast were accomplished in 1968. On 17 December 1968, a successful first rocket launching was fired at St. Lucia Bay.

In 1969, Defence Minister Botha announced that South Africa had developed the Cactus air defence system in cooperation with the French. This system has been the backbone for South African air defence until recently.

The growth of South Africa's arms industry, and the continuation of its *apartheid* policy through the 1960's, created a climate in the international community that was eventually to lead to a United Nations mandatory arms embargo in 1977.

The Debate

On 4 December 1963, the United Nations Security Council unanimously approved a resolution calling for an embargo on equipment for making arms and asking Secretary General U Thant to name a small group of experts to seek peaceful solutions to apartheid. France and Great Britian joined the vote but refused to ban defensive arms for South Africa. Ambassador Stevenson, United States, backed the resolution. Security Council Resolution (SCR) 181 of 7 August 1963 called for all UN members to ban all arms shipments to South Africa. On 4 December 1963 the so-called 'voluntary arms embargo' under SCR 182 was unanimously approved by the Council. During the debate before SCR 182 was adopted, numerous heated arguments took place within the Assembly.

On 13 February 1963 the Afro-Asian People's Solidarity Conference castigated Great Britain and France for supplying arms to South Africa.[2] This was followed by a verbal attack on France by the Pan-African Congress representative, Mr. Duncan. He charged that South Africa enforced apartheid principally through arms supplied chiefly by France. At the same time, a United Nations commission charged that Great Britain, the United States, Spain and many other nations were supplying arms to South Africa.[3] Ghana's Ambassador Quaison-Sackey demanded that the United Nations should exclude South Africa from membership.[4]

As Britain was feeling pressure from the Third World countries and at home, the Foreign Secretary, Sir Alec Douglas Home, in a carefully worded statement, said that Great Britain would oppose the sale of arms to be used to enforce apartheid but would honour any and all commitments to sell weapons for defence.[5]

The Afro-Asian bloc called on the Security Council for a complete trade boycott and arms embargo to force an end of the existing racial policies. Ghana, Morocco and the Philippines were in the vanguard. At the same time, Soviet ambassador Fedorenko urged the ouster of RSA from the UN.[6] As an adjunct to Fedorenko's move, the Afro-Asian bloc called on the Security Council for a complete arms embargo by way of a resolution.[7] As the debate thickened, the African Unity Organisation Foreign Ministers scorned the United States, Britain and France for the stands they had taken during the Council debates.[8] The debate continued and as the tempo of the pressure from the international community increased, a United Nations commission urged member states to bar any arms to South Africa and refrain from training their military personnel.[9] Caught in the web of the polemics of member states, United State's decided to ban export licences for commercial arms shipments to South Africa by 1964.[10]

While G. Mennen Williams, Assistant Secretary of State for African Affairs was insisting that the United State's should extend its arms ban against South Africa to all arms, except those under existing contracts and 'those which might be required in the interests of world peace',[11] the Israelis, recipients of large amounts of American aid (currently $1.8 billion annually), were formulating a 'joint arms industry' with South Africa.[12] According to Jane Hunter, since the first arms embargo of 1963, Armscor, in its quest to obtain arms and develop an arms industry, has received Israeli assistance and does so still.[13] It is worth noting that William Minter believes that the costliest international sanctions imposed on South Africa are the oil and arms embargoes, despite loopholes and evasion.[14] He states:

> The UN arms bans, voluntary since 1963 and mandatory since 1977, have also hurt Pretoria, even though they were adopted by Western powers largely for reasons of international image rather than as a serious effort to cut down South Africa's military potential ... a House Foreign Affairs Africa Subcommittee study [concluded] in March 1982

that there was a 'non-system of enforcing the arms embargo in the US government.' The British arms ban also contains many loopholes, which have allowed, for example, the export of sophisticated military radar systems because they can also be used for civilian purposes.

Yet embargo-breaking has been expensive. The cost of evading sanctions probably represents a substantial proportion of South Africa's annual arms procurement budget, estimated at as much as $800-million. Furthermore, despite South Africa's claim that the arms embargo has helped stimulate its domestic arms industry, Pretoria still cannot produce the most advanced weapons systems. Most of its heavy equipment still comes from the West and some of it is more than 20 years old.[15]

Obviously, this flies in the face of a long series of statements by American policy makers pertaining to the United State's adherence to the United Nations arms embargoes. It had its genesis in the Security Council when the late Ambassador Stevenson, announcing the arms ban in 1963 said:

> The United States as a nation with many responsibilities in many parts of the world, naturally reserves the right in the future to interpret this policy in the light of requirements for assuring the maintenance of international peace and security. If the interests of the world community

PLATE 2.1 Impala Aircraft

PLATE 2.2   Silvermine Communications Centre

require the provision of equipment for use in the common defence effort, we would naturally feel able to do so without violating the spirit and the intent of this resolve.[16]

This open-ended statement could very well have led to a loose interpretation of United State's intent which prompted The House of Representatives Foreign Affairs Africa Subcommittee to state there was a 'non-system of enforcing the arms embargo in the U.S. government'.[17] Furthermore, G. Mennen Williams, in his testimony in 1966 before the Subcommittee, cited the regulations governing the Department of Commerce enforcement of the arms embargo as contained in part 373.66 of the United States Department of Commerce Comprehensive Export Schedule as such:

> In reconsidering the application to export or requests to re-export any commodity to the Republic of South Africa, the policy of the Office of Export Control is generally to deny applications covering arms, munitions, military vehicles, or items used primarily in the manufacture or maintenance of arms, munitions, or implements of war.[18]

The Schedule provided flexibility for policy makers and other 'interpreters' of American intent by specifically using the phrase '... is generally to deny applications.' On Wednesday, 2 March 1966, the Honourable

Alexander Trowbridge, Assistant Secretary of Commerce for Domestic and International Business testified before the same subcommittee. In response to a question by the Chairman, Congressman Barratt O'Hara, on a plan to sell air equipment to South Africa, Trowbridge stated:

> There have been a number of applications, Mr Chairman, for permits to export aircraft to the Republic of South Africa. Licencing of military aircraft is under the jurisdiction of the Office of Munitions Control of the Department of State. Military aircraft are denied licences in accordance with the UN Security Council resolutions which have dealt with the questions of arms, ammunition, and military equipment. Most civilian aircraft is licenced for export by the Department of Commerce. In implementing the UN arms embargo, the Department of Commerce has denied licences for the sale of civilian aircraft to South Africa where it was determined that the aircraft would likely be used for military purposes. There have been other cases where the end use was of a purely commercial nature and the export has not been prevented.[19]

Additional questioning from Congressman Benjamin S. Rosenthal indicated the fine line that exists in interpreting the then existing policy of the Office of Export Control.

> *Mr. Rosenthal*: Are you familiar with the program of a Michigan concern which is building a $550,000 plant for light aircraft which claims to have a 90-foot takeoff, a four-seater plane, to be used by the South African police?
> *Mr. Trowbridge*: I am not familiar with that; no, sir.
> *Mr. Rosenthal*: I will give you the name of the company, and where they are from in Michigan, but taking the prohibition you yourself suggested, I am reluctant to do that publicly. I will give it to you afterward, and I would ask if you would look into it and let me have the details. Thank you, Mr Chairman.[20]

Defence Co-operation

As South Africa continued to develop its defence strategy in the light of SCR 182, its initial defence strategy of preserving internal security expanded to include preserving stability in the Southern African region. If one examines the size and capability of the South African Defence Force, one can readily come to the conclusion of its ability to concentrate forces rapidly and overwhelm point targets. However, in the light of controlling internal situations, border infiltrations, and stepped-up insurgent activities, the South African forces would indeed be overstretched by a major confrontation. In order to ensure that a major confrontation with neighbouring states is minimised, it has become vital that South Africa ensures that its neighbours do not support insurgencies that are contrary to the republic. In so doing it has employed both pre-emptive military tactical strikes and sophisticated economic pressures. This is so in the view of Abdul Minty when he points out, '... the fact that South Africa has a very "low security ceiling".'[21]

From a geostrategic view, when the diminished British defence role included its withdrawal from 'East of Suez', the United States, eager to fill the vacuum in the Indian Ocean area, pushed for an expansion of base facilities at the British owned island in the Indian Ocean, Diego Garcia. In addition, there was high level defence co-operation between the United States and South Africa. Abdul Minty follows on this theme when he talks about the Advokaat System:

> A major aspect of this developing Western alliance with South Africa is the construction of the Advokaat military communications system by South Africa in co-operation with several Western companies at a cost of R15-million. The installation became operational in March 1973 and is claimed to be the most modern system of its kind with the ability to maintain surveillance from South Africa's coastline across the South Atlantic to South America and across the Indian Ocean to Australia and New Zealand. The headquarters of this system is at Silvermine, Westlake, which is near Cape Town and not far from the Simonstown Naval Base. It has several sub-stations, including one in Walvis Bay in Namibia, and reported, it is directly linked by permanent channels with 'the Royal Navy in Whitehall' and 'with the US Navy base at San Juan in Puerto Rico.'[22]

In the 1950s and early 1960s, most of South Africa's weapons systems were of British origin with a mixture of American aircraft. 'By the early 1960s the flow of armaments from Britain and the USA into South Africa was well established.'[23] Ostensibly, according to the International Defence and Aid Fund, the military-industrial complex of South Africa began well before the 1977 mandatory arms embargo:

> In 1964, with assistance from private industry, two state organisations were established: the Armaments Board, for purchasing arms and maintaining quality and cost control in production, and the Armaments Development and Production Corporation (Armscor), the controlling body for armaments manufacture. A third body, the National Institute

for Defence Research (NIDR) had been formed in the 1950s under the wing of the Council for Scientific and Industrial Research to be responsible for all weapons research and development. In 1967 a special committee was appointed to investigate various armaments organisations abroad and subsequently the French 'DMA' military-industrial system was chosen as a model for the development of the South African arms industry.[24]

Acting from Strength

Armscor only comes into the arms procurement and manufacturing picture after the Defence Force has determined what specific weapons systems are needed to defend South Africa in accordance with policy laid down through the State President to the Defence Minister. The expansion of existing lines, similar to the Centurian/Oliphant tank, and of course, the cost factor, have a heavy bearing in the determination of systems to be procured.

'Through a joint committee, they (SADF) state their needs relative to the external threat, then we state our capabilities of meeting these needs within cost and time limits'.[25] The NIDR has played an important part in missile development from the early 1950s to the late 1960s. The French-South African scientific connection reached its apex when South African scientists designed the Crotale surface-to-air missile (also known as CACTUS). Subsequently, the missile was manufactured in France by Thomson CSF.[26] Kentron and Lyttleton Engineering works now are responsible for the manufacture and development of missiles. It can readily be assumed that missile production in South Africa would not be at its present state of sophistication had it not been for the arms embargo coupled with external source help.

Regardless of the arguments presented on the self-sufficiency of South Africa in armaments, the degree is fairly high. If trends continue Armscor 'will clearly continue to provide a comprehensive arsenal for the SADF'.[27] With increasing budgetary expenditures the 'military-industrial complex' as well as 'the military effort is clearly penetrating the South African economy as well as the machinery of government'.[28]

As the perception of total isolation becomes more imminent, representatives of South Africa reiterate their theme that South Africa must act from strength to counter the classical communist recipe which, according to General Malan, has four distinct phases; political agitation, terrorism, guerrilla warfare and the transition of guerrilla

PLATE 2.3   Cactus Surface-to-Air Missile System

warfare into conventional war. This line of reasoning continues to hammer home the theme that terrorists try to drive a wedge between the people and the government and a peaceful solution is not in the schema of the African National Congress (ANC), terrorism will not be tolerated and furthermore, no organisation will be permitted to operate outside the law.[29] As an adjunct to this theme a constant reminder as to the threat the Soviets pose to the southern oceans and harbours, namely the strategic importance of the Cape sea route, are quoted in the South African press.[30]

As the *laager* is forced to draw tighter in the light of the arms embargo and economic sanctions, the demonstrable response of the Republic has been perplexing in some international circles. The South Africans have the technical know-how and will to manufacture practically anything and this has been shown vividly with its SASOL oil-from-coal plants which can supply over 70 per cent of their liquid fuel needs. On the other hand, Armscor now exports arms to 26 countries and its finest self-propelled G6 nuclear-capable howitzer has been reported to be in action in Iraq.[31] One may wonder why constant and continuous attention is directed toward South Africa when, according to Peter Brimelow, South Africa is actually a poor country.

PLATE 2.4   G6 Howitzer

Its total gross national product is only $51 billion, one-third of Australia's and 1% of the U.S., a mere $2,232 per capita. That's not enough to go round. The whites, 19.3% of the population and possessors of all the vital technical skills, already contribute 93% of income tax revenue and pay European levels of tax. South Africa is a microcosm of the world – except that its First World is taxed to subsidise its Third World.[32]

Notwithstanding the unequal distribution of income, the answer may lie in the fact that South Africa is an enigma and statistics are but one piece of the puzzle. The political, economic and social dimensions are as complex as any within the international community but are frequently viewed in many circles as black and/or white. Unfortunately, these oversimplifications are used as a device to explain phenomena. For example, the Republic of South Africa must be viewed as the dominant player in Southern Africa not as a strategic player in the Western view of the world. However, South Africa's minerals are germane to any geostrategic question only in so far as these minerals are cost effective for the West to purchase *vis-à-vis* using substitutes, or being at the mercy of the Soviet Union extractive mineral industry.

'Marshmallow' Embargoes

According to Sean Gervasi in his July 1977 testimony before the subcommittee on Africa of the House of Representatives Committee on International Relations, there was at that time 'extensive evidence of the breakdown of the voluntary arms embargo. ... The United States in particular ... appeared to have shipped large numbers of major weapons systems ... to South Africa.'[33] It appeared that most of the violations took place in the 1970s. It becomes important to note at this juncture that South Africa continued 'to import 55 per cent of its arms requirements'.[34] Sean Gervasi continues to show the futility of a voluntary arms embargo when he says:

> Thus secret United States arms sales to South Africa have involved a new kind of triangular trade. Weapons licenced for production in other countries, and controlled by the Office of Munitions Control in the Department of State, have been transferred directly or through dealers from the foreign licencees to South Africa. Other countries besides the United States have thus become guilty of violating the 1963 embargo by virtue of their co-operation in these practices. Many important sales to South Africa, it will be seen, made use of Italian licencees as intermediaries.[35]

Although Sean Gervasi was claiming that South Africa needed 'to import 55 per cent of its arms requirements', Mr. P.W. Botha, then Minister of Defence, thought otherwise when he announced in the House of Assembly on 26 April 1972 the progress being made in the development of advanced type of ammunition and armaments:

> I want to repeat today that South Africa can no longer be isolated by arms boycotts. We are absolutely self-sufficient regarding internal demands – on the contrary, an intensive investigation is under way at present with a view to exporting such weaponry.[36]

Paul Johnson, British political commentator, author and historian believes that a sophisticated modern state such as South Africa is 'extraordinarily impervious to economic sanctions'.[37] On the surface, it is difficult to fault his argument if one accepts the premise that the two decade-old arms embargo has led to the creation of an almost self-sufficient arms industry. As previously mentioned, similar results have been attained through the oil embargo in the development of a South African synthetic fuel industry. Along this line of reasoning, Johnson states:

> Not only has the country made itself 85 per cent self-sufficient in energy but it has, as a by-product, modernised and expanded its coal industry

to create the lowest-cost coal-export trade in the world. ... The truth is, the administrative difficulties free-world governments now find in controlling capital movements across frontiers are almost insuperable.[38]

If indeed, controlling capital movements across frontiers is well nigh improbable then the Israelis 'phase-out of existing agreements on arms sales and the transfer of technology to South Africa'[39] will probably take considerable time in the light of numerous existing non-military joint ventures such as uranium for nuclear power development, Israeli imports of coal and steel as well as the importation of uncut diamonds. This annual $160 million two-way trade (not including military transfers to South Africa, which is a state secret) as well as arms technology are the underpinnings for Israeli-South African relations. In March 1987, the Israelis publicly announced a phase out of providing technology and arms sales to South Africa while continuing to honour agreements regarding the transfer of military technology and expertise that are still in effect since the 1960s, thereby continuing large-scale funding of Israeli research and development projects for the trade of licences with the attendant know-how to South Africa. This entrenched symbiotic relationship is difficult, at best, to sever rapidly without consequences that the Israelis are unwilling to accept. The only measure that would ensure a total Israeli-compliance with the arms embargo would be a drastic cut in the annual appropriation of American aid. This, however, is highly unlikely due to the internal political ramifications within the United States Government.

The 1977 United Nations Mandatory Arms Embargo

The 1977 United Nations mandatory arms embargo was designed to stop the procurement of arms by South Africa. The thinking behind the United Nations actions was that if Pretoria had no means of procuring arms, South Africa could no longer pursue its political objectives aggressively through its military and police. However, the opposite occurred. South Africa channelled its efforts into its own arms industry, manufacturing an array of weapons systems.

The apartheid policy of South Africa was regarded in the international political arena as unacceptable. This internal policy of 'slavery' was the basis for the United Nations decreeing the compulsory regulation of an arms embargo. *Apartheid* is seen as a 'violation of human rights and as a crime against the human race'. This 'infringement of international law' in terms of Chapter Seven of the United Nations Charter was based on South Africa's military build-up which was used as a threat to neighbouring states and a threat to international peace and stability. Because of this, all states were enjoined to observe strictly the arms embargo against South Africa.

In 1973, the United Nations requested member states to consider the situation in South Africa with a view to adopting effective measures. By 1975, a compulsory arms embargo against South Africa was requested in terms of Chapter Seven of the United Nations Charter. This move was of historical significance as it was the first time that actions in terms of Chapter Seven had been requested. However, dissenting votes in the Security Council blocked the measure. The call within the General Assembly for an arms embargo became more formulated and methodical. Three inter-related events were directly responsible for the concerted efforts of the General Assembly. First, South Africa continued its weapons build-up; second, South Africa blatantly interfered in the internal affairs of Angola in 1975/76; and third, South African administration and military presence in South West Africa/Namibia was in violation of United Nations Resolution 2145 of 27 October 1966.

Since 1962 there had been various attempts to institute a compulsory arms embargo against South Africa. The 1963 Resolutions 181 and 182 dealt with the sale of armaments to the Republic and the detention of political prisoners under apartheid law. Resolution 418 of 1977 corresponded closely to the Lagos Declaration against apartheid, in that it called for the cessation of all arms and military assistance to South Africa, the full implementation of an arms embargo, and called for non-co-operation of member states in sporting contacts with South Africa.

The attitude towards South Africa reflected by the United Nations in 1977 was buttressed by resolutions citing the 1976 Soweto riots, deteriorating human rights and wanton killings. Predictably, in 1977, Resolution 418 was adopted condemning South Africa for apartheid and attacks against neighbouring states. In addition, the resolution decided that all states should cease providing South Africa with any type of military equipment and licences. Resolution 421, adopted in December 1977, formed a committee to monitor the implementation of Resolution 418, known as Security Council Committee 421.

Three main problem areas centred on Resolution 418 namely, contravention of the embargo through third parties, legislation adopted by states was often ambiguous and vague, and large scale confusion resulted from the different interpretation of the wording of the Resolution. Numerous recommendations to close 'loopholes' were made by Committee 421 resulting in Resolution 558 of 1984 which strengthened the arms embargo. Although Resolution 558 is not mandatory it does recognise South Africa's ability to produce arms and places a moral duty on states to refrain from importing arms from South Africa.

Changing South African Politico-Military Strategy

By the 1970s there had emerged four main areas of threat against the security of South Africa – insurgent action, conventional assault, economic suasion and psychological warfare. The ANC increased its ability to carry out military actions from four guerrilla attacks in 1976 to over 136 armed actions in 1985 according to the *East London Daily Dispatch* (12 Jan 86).

Pretoria considers that the increasing range, quantity and degree of sophistication of armaments from the Soviet bloc to Angola, Mozambique, the ANC and the South West African People's Organisation (SWAPO) provide the weapon capacity for the conduct of conventional war against the South African Republic. Of increasing concern was the economic threat posed by international trade action and linked to the internal campaign of black unions moving toward the maximum amount of economic disruption. This was considered to be more of a potent threat than insurgent action.

Compounding the thrust against South Africa, in Pretoria's view, was a relentless psychological warfare campaign orchestrated by the Soviet Union and its satellites. This campaign to isolate the Republic from the international community has been increasingly effective. Moreover, it is assisted in part by the communications media throughout the world, government agencies, international fora and the United Nations. It is intended to condition the world toward further economic and military hostile action against South Africa.

The aim of this concerted effort is to break their will to resist. Thus, Pretoria fears, South Africa will eventually fall under the Marxist sphere of influence. These combined forms of threat, in Pretoria's view, constitute the 'total onslaught' against South Africa.

To meet the threat the Republic has devised a 'total strategy'. This strategy has its underpinnings based on the unique political, economic, social and military structure within the country. They believe that global conceptual interpretations of concepts such as 'one person, one vote' and 'majority rule' have little relevance in Africa. History has shown, they claim, that when and if applied to South Africa, the result could very well be catastrophic.

South Africa sees herself as being in conflict with Soviet expansionism. Pretoria has adopted an offensive strategy which includes military pre-emptive strikes or hot pursuit. In the face of military, economic and psychological onslaught only a comprehensive counterstrategy, they claim, will enable the Republic to survive. In their view, a sound political strategy is the key to long term stability. With this philosophy in mind, Pretoria has organised its defence establishment accordingly. Furthermore, government opinion makers publicly state that if South Africa is economically destabilised, then the economic structure of the whole of Southern Africa will be torn asunder and the vital strategic interests of the West placed in jeopardy.

The first indications of a positive movement towards a 'total response' was a movement toward a unified state security doctrine contained in the 1970 Potgieter Commission Inquiry Report which suggested the establishment of a centralised intelligence agency (BOSS). In 1972, a State Security Council was formed as a result of the report. The internecine struggle of Prime Minister Vorster's power base in BOSS and the military establishment under P.W. Botha was such that the State Security Council was unable to fulfil its coordinating role. This power struggle led to P.W. Botha presenting the March 1975 Defence White Paper to parliament which, among other positions, laid out a defence strategy for the defence establishment that was considerably more than military strategy. The White Paper asserted:

> It involves economy, ideology, technology, and even social matters and can therefore only be meaningful and valid if proper account is taken of these other spheres ... all countries must, more than ever, muster all their activities – political, economic, diplomatic and military – for their defence. This, in fact, is the meaning of 'Total Strategy.'[40]

A unified national security doctrine was spelt out in the 1977 Defence White Paper, triggered to a great degree by the previous Soweto uprisings and Pretoria's isolation following South Africa's invasion of Angola. In the White Paper every aspect of the state was deemed to be the legitimate concern of the South African Defence Forces. Therefore, the 1977 Defence White Paper widely broadened the concept of state security to include all aspects of society.

A reliable system of policy-making and implementation integrated with the military and intelligence communities started in earnest in September 1979. Various ad hoc cabinet committees which had operated under the Vorster administration were abolished. In April 1980, thirty-nine government departments were reduced to twenty-two and the Office of the Prime Minister was enlarged to include six planning divisions. The decentralisation and rearrangement of state functions facilitated a power structure known as the National Security Management System (NSMS). The NSMS has virtually taken over the formulation and execution of government policy.

A reaffirmation of the National Party's basic principles were contained in P.W. Botha's August 1979 Twelve Point Plan which stressed integrating the military into the process of administration.

The State Security Council (SSC) of the National Security Management System has absolute power to make and implement decisions relating to state security. The SSC has clearly usurped many of the functions of the cabinet. The armed forces play a decisive role in the Council. Directly under the SSC are fifteen interdepartmental committees (IDCs) which are responsible for national coordination of the total strategy. Joint Management Centres (JMCs) are tasked with regional implementation of the strategy. The Council is chaired by the President. It has been created by law and deals with a much broader range of issues than any other cabinet committees. Of ominous importance in implementing Pretoria's strategy is that a committee of the SSC has the responsibility of coordinating the activities of South Africa's three intelligence agencies.

By the early 1970s Pretoria was convinced that it would have to become self-sufficient in arms production if it were to survive. This conviction was in light of the foregoing and of increasing support by the international community for the arms embargo, the internal threat of insurgency in South Africa, and the possibility of a regional war. To meet the country's varying armaments needs and develop the local capacity for doing so, Armscor's terms of reference were simple and direct; involve the private sector 'effectively and economically' in the execution of this task.

The imposition of the total arms boycott on South Africa on 4 November 1977, provided powerful impetus to Armscor and had a dramatic impact on its procurement function. In 1978/79, 6,494 contracts to the value of R1,742 million were concluded with suppliers – despite the boycott. The following year, the number of contracts increased to nearly 9,000.

In 1981, one of the world's most advanced nitro-cellulose plants was commissioned by Somchem at Krantzkop, near Wellington.

In 1981, Armscor made a decision that was to change the scope and capacity from meeting the country's armaments needs to expanding into the international market. This was brought about by a period of consolidation. The race to support the defence forces with weapons had succeeded. To effectively maintain its production line and the expertise that had been built up over the years, Armscor had to produce at a level over the needs of the defence forces. Therefore, in 1982, Armscor entered the international arms market. This, undoubtedly, was a new chapter in Armscor's development. Success in the international market aided Armscor in becoming a major earner of valuable foreign exchange for South Africa.

Due to the nature of the threat, Armscor had no need to develop nuclear submarines, intermediate-range ballistic missiles, or similar costly and time-consuming weapons. Relatively simple infantry and artillery weapons, light strike aircraft and armoured vehicles could be manufactured to counter the threat. There was little hope of manufacturing weapons that were quantitatively superior due to the Soviet Bloc's infusion of weaponry into southern Africa. Thus, South Africa concentrated on qualitatively superior weapons which not only aided the defence forces but gained credibility in the international arms community. Therefore, the research and development effort was concentrated in a concise area. It is estimated that the proceeds from Armscor's international arms sales in 1987 and 1988 will fund the necessary research for development for the next generation.

Armscor, the controlling body for a confederation of companies, is intent on expanding its share of the international market. In doing so, however, they have not lost sight that national security is their aim, and the priority for their armaments industry is geared toward this end.

A number of world opinion makers contributed to the 1977 United Nations mandatory arms embargo. Realising the failure of the voluntary embargo of 1963, the forces behind the 1977 one realised that a mandatory embargo, although far from being the answer was a better attempt than heretofore. In fact, United States regulations are more severe than the dictates of the 1977 mandatory arms embargo in that they restrict items of export to the South African Defence Force and police that are not covered in the United Nations embargo.[40] However, United States policy stipulates that prospective computer sales are examined on a case-by-case basis to ensure that they do not enhance the capability of South Africa's security forces. Nevertheless, computers were not denied to other agencies because to do so 'would not lessen the ability of the South African Government to enforce *apartheid*'.[41] Chester A. Crocker, Assistant Secretary of State for African Affairs, testifying before the House of Representatives Committee on Foreign Affairs on 17 April 1985, reiterated an earlier theme that the arms embargo was not showing expected results.

> Experience with the United Nations arms embargo against South Africa shows that it has not had the crippling effect on South Africa's military capability as desired. Indeed, it has provided the impetus to turn South Africa into the 10th largest armaments manufacturer in the world. While we doubt that South Africa could still build up its electronics industry fast enough to overcome immediately any computer and software ban from the United States, given South Africa's proven ability to develop self-sufficiency and the ability of other nations to replace the United States as a supplier of computers, a unilateral ban on the export of computers to South Africa by the United States would, in the long term, do much more harm to the United States than to South Africa.[42]

Not only had South Africa been able to stymie the arms embargo, it began an arms export drive in earnest in the Greek Defendory Expo

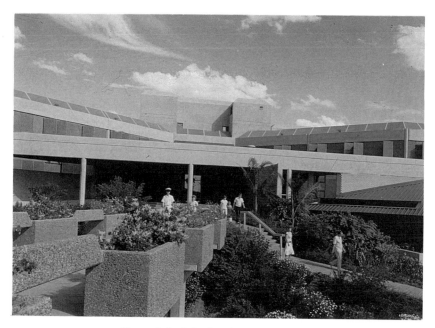

PLATE 2.5   Infoplan Computer Centre

in 1982 which was the result of a decision by Pretoria 'to approve a major effort to increase foreign sales'.[43] Two years after being asked to leave the international arms show in Athens, Armscor exhibited military electronics, ordnance and missiles at the FIDA '84 armaments show in Santiago, Chile. Part of this drive to export was the result of Armscor's capacity being cut in half because of a reduction in orders caused by the cessation of the Rhodesian war, the reduction of large scale offensive operations in Angola and a drawdown on hostile incidents against the South West African People's Organisation (SWAPO) along the Namibian/Angola border.

No One's Military Client

For any industry to remain viable it cannot afford large production swings. Of concern was Armscor's amortisation of its large investment in research and development and the retention of its highly trained technical personnel. The confidence of industry officials when speaking on South Africa's reaction to any export ban on arms is extraordinary. 'We will get round any UN ban on our exports just like we got around the ban on imports.'[44] Nevertheless, aware of political sensitivities, South African firms manufacturing military equipment frequently market their products through third parties via companies, particularly in Western Europe. South Africa is prepared to export at least twenty-seven weapons systems with a built-in logistic tail of spare parts, technical training and advice necessary to keep these sophisticated armaments functioning effectively and efficiently. The facts readily support a South Africa that is not the military client of anyone but one seeking clients to purchase armaments. Chester Crocker brought this out vividly in his testimony before the House of Representatives Subcommittee on International Economic Policy and Trade on Africa when being questioned by Congressman Ted Weiss from New York.

Mr. Crocker: One of the reasons that South Africa is able to operate with such independence in the military field is that it is not the military client of anyone and that's a fact.

Mr. Weiss: Before you respond then, let me just comment on that. I was going to take note of the fact that, in your prepared statement and as you delivered it to us, you take great credit for American sanctions that are in place. However, in your asides you have, in fact, been criticising those very sanctions that you take credit for and it seems to

PLATE 2.6   Ratel 12.7 mm Armoured Personnel Carrier

PLATE 2.7   Hippo Armoured Vehicles

PLATE 2.8   Samil 20 Bulldog APC

PLATE 2.9   Samil 100 Transporter

me that you're making a marvellous effort at being on both sides of the issue.

Mr. Crocker: No, not at all. What I am saying is that we applied the law, we have a policy and we think it is the right policy of distancing from South Africa's security apparatus, but let's not kid ourselves about the effects of that distancing in practical terms. That's what I am saying.

Mr. Weiss: So that it's OK for those sanctions that are in place, even though they have negative consequences, but you don't want any new ones?

Mr. Crocker: Well, if there is a mood in the Congress to have a serious look at the repeal of the arms embargo against South Africa, then we might be able to have a constructive discussion as to the terms for the repeal of the arms embargo, but I don't sense that that is the mood of Congress.

Mr. Weiss: I just want to know where you're coming from. That's all.[45]

Crocker's assessment was based on the fact that South Africa is able to design, develop, technologically test and put in the field new weapons systems despite the arms embargo. In addition, Pretoria has ready access to commercially produced, technologically advanced products from the international market place. Many of these systems can be classified as dual purpose and have direct military applications such as computers discussed above. Modern weapons systems require high technological components based on sophisticated electronics, communications, optics and a vast array of state-of-the-art technologically advanced subsystems.

As the 1985 South African Computer User's Handbook stated:

> Direct sales to South African weapons manufacturers have persisted despite the UN embargo. Mohawk Data systems equipment is used by Kentron, the Armscor subsidiary that makes guided missiles; Eloptro, which specialises in military electro-optics; and Somchem, which outfits the South African Defence Force with propellants and explosives. Another affiliate, Naschem, was on record as using a Hewlett-Packard Company computer in 1982, and the Reagan Administration authorised the sale of a Sperry computer to Armscor's Atlas Aircraft in 1981. Direct exports to Armscor are now prohibited under U.S. regulations, but the South Africans have apparently been able to keep the supply lines open.[46]

The relationship between the Council for Scientific and Industrial Research (CSIR) and the South African Armed Forces and police can easily be ascertained without being knowledgeable about detail. For

PLATE 2.10   Eloptro

PLATE 2.11   Somchem

PLATE 2.12   Naschem

instance, it is a matter of record that CSIR is involved in missile design options, target acquisition methods and communication signal research for the army and security-related research, like fingerprinting storage access programmes, for the police.

In 1982, Bophuthatswana and Ciskei, 'homelands' within South Africa, acquired military systems, particularly light aircraft through South Africa which were transhipped from the United States or Israel. Helio-Courier planes from America went to Bophuthatswana and light aircraft from the Mooney Company in America went to Ciskei via Israel.[47] Britain, West Germany and Japan have provided systems for use in security from mobile military radar to computers, to powerpacks and chassis used in the 155 millimetre howitzer artillery system and the 127 millimetre Valkiri missile system. Firms such as Magirus-Deutz, Unimog, Maschinenfabrik-Augsburg-Nurnburg and Siemens have played prominent roles in supplying South Africa. With components, subsystems, technology and licencing coming from an array of various source-countries, the direct task of policing and enforcing any type of arms embargo becomes not only exceptionally difficult but futile in the light of diverse political ideologies and economic incentives of suppliers in the international arena. As an example, the licencing process, which is overseen by the United States

PLATE 2.13   Valkiri Rocket System

Commerce and State Departments, works from a Commodity Control List which contains dual-use equipment and general commodities. This catalogue lists those items that are deemed strategically, techno-logically and militarily significant such as electronics, communication equipment, computers and a various assortment of spares. Computers are rapidly becoming the mainstay of technologically sophisticated weapons systems. In 1984, American companies sold $185 million worth of computers and related software to South Africa. These computer-related sales were more than all other countries' exports to South Africa combined.[48] Thomas Conrad, with the research unit of the American Friends Service Committee in Philadelphia, gives a graphic illustration of the frustration with the arms embargo as demonstrated by the United States State Department Munitions List.

> The ... munitions list encompasses many articles not covered by the embargo, and the United States will only consider applications for such items not covered by the embargo, a U.S. official stated at the United Nations on October 23, 1984. Munitions List exports have therefore jumped dramatically.
>
> In virtual secrecy, the State Department licenced over $27.9 million worth of technology on the Munitions List for export to South Africa from 1982 to 1984, according to information obtained by the American

Friends Service Committee under the Freedom of Information Act. The sales included encryption equipment, navigation gear, image intensifiers, and technical know-how.[49]

Conrad goes on to state that the regulations have 'several blind spots', namely the advance contract signing measure, foreign assembled systems with less than 20 per cent cost of United States supplied parts, sales to peripheral organisations connected to Armscor that are not totally banned, and sales from the Commodity Control List and Munitions List that are permitted or are not completely banned.[50]

The Contrary Body of Evidence

There is a contrary body of evidence that suggests that an effective arms embargo will have a crippling effect on South Africa. These effects have been fuelled by major strains on the operational capacity of the armed forces because of 'aggression' against the Frontline States, the insurgency in Namibia, and the unrest in townships and rural areas. The International Seminar on the United Nations arms embargo against South Africa held in London on 28–30 May 1986 makes a case for South Africa's external dependency on military armaments.

> The seminar was provided with a thorough assessment of the *apartheid* regime's capacity to produce and procure armaments. It found that the South African armed forces are highly dependent on external sources of supply for much of [their] main armaments. It further established that, contrary to the *apartheid* regime's claims, which appeared to enjoy wide-spread acceptance in various international circles, it was in fact not self-sufficient in the production of its arms and related materials of all types. In several key areas it is more dependent today on external supply of components, spares and other items than before and is therefore, even more vulnerable to an effective arms embargo.[51]

If these assertions are correct, then the 'widespread acceptance in various international circles' is an extraordinary attempt at misinformation from internal South African sources and external investigatory journalism from various authors. In all probability the truth lies somewhere between the claims of the Republic of South African Government and those who are at the forefront of pushing the enforcement of the mandatory arms embargo. Nevertheless, Pretoria has shown resilience, flexibility, initiative and an exceptional capacity for circumventive manoeuvring in the past, so one can readily expect this same type of track record in the future. Because of the political, socio-economic and security structure of the RSA, it is relatively less difficult to mobilise segments within this society for specific purposes. The case in point being Armscor whose government mandated umbrella covers all armaments procurement, testing and manufacture. When monies, capacity, technological competence, expertise and zeal can be specifically directed toward an end, the likelihood of success is obviously greatly enhanced. Hence the story of Armscor and its successful 'end run' against mandatory sanctions. The World Conference on Sanctions Against Racist South Africa, held in Paris on 16–20 June 1986, recommended strong reinforcement of SCR 418 of 4 November 1977 (mandatory arms embargo) by calling upon all States 'to end all military and nuclear collaboration with South Africa' and an assortment of other measures designed to elicit more co-operation of States 'to cease the sale or supply of "dual-purpose" items ...' and 'to terminate all investments in corporations manufacturing military equipment ... in South Africa.' The World Conference directly sought Security Council action in armament exports and to strengthen the mandatory arms embargo:

> The World Conference further urges the Security Council to make mandatory its request to all States, in paragraph 2 of its resolution 558 (1984) of 13 December 1984, 'to refrain from importing arms,

PLATE 2.14   120, 250 and 460 kilogram Bombs

PLATE 2.15   Ammunition from Armscor Factories

ammunition of all types and military vehicles produced in South Africa'
and to extend the embargo to cover all components and related material
originating from South Africa.

The World Conference welcomes the declaration of the International
Seminar on Arms Embargo against South Africa (A/41/388-S/1821,
annex), held in London from 28 to 30 May 1986, and believes that it is
imperative that the measures recommended therein be taken to reinforce
and strengthen the mandatory arms embargo by the Security Council
in Resolution 418 (1977).[52]

In their concluding remarks, the International Seminar stressed the
importance of the mandatory arms embargo which 'has created
serious shortages for the South African military forces and deprived
them of certain vital supplies'.[53] The Seminar praised the majority of
member states in the United Nations for their vigilance and prompt
action in this affair. However, it mildly castigated other members by
stating, 'If all states exercised similar vigilance, the results could be
far-reaching and make much of the South African Defence Force
inoperative.'[54] At times, conflicting signals are given by the South
Africans who seem to agree with conclusions of the International
Seminar and World Conference on the one hand, yet turn around
and disagree on the other. For example, the following direct sequential

PLATE 2.16   40 mm 6-Shot Grenade Launcher

PLATE 2.17   Samil 20 Office Vehicle

PLATE 2.18   Samil 20 Rhino and Samil 20 Personnel Carrier

quotes are taken from the *White Paper on Defence and Armaments Supply*, 1986:

> 154. The arms embargo, as contained in Resolution 418 of the Security Council of the UN, was implemented more than eight years ago and is still being applied with great enthusiasm and *increasing effectiveness*.

> 155. The security forces of the RSA are consequently at present totally dependent on the local arms industry for their changing and diverse needs. *Had Armscor not been able to establish this industry, the arms embargo would have succeeded in its aim,* and the military threats could have been truly demoralising and the terror attacks possibly crippling.*[55]

As a matter of record, a committee was appointed in 1984 by the RSA to conduct an in-depth investigation of the structure of the South African Defence Force. This Committee was to take an in-depth view on whether the defence establishment (in this case Armscor and the Defence Force) could meet the short term future 'demands and requirements of an effective armed force'. The Committee found that ... 'the SADF and Armscor are capable of meeting the present

---

*Author's emphasis.

requirements and that only slight adjustments would be required in order to meet the challenges of the future'.[56]

It has become apparent that some of the 'slight adjustments', 'in order to meet the challenges of the future', might have come from the United States' Western European allies in the North Atlantic Treaty Organisation. France, Britian, West Germany, Italy and Switzerland (Switzerland is not a NATO member) have been providing arms to Pretoria despite the mandatory arms embargo.*[57]

Conclusion

South Africa is militarily better prepared than at any time in its history. However, this is not to conclude that the forces opposed to the Republic will not eventually reach their goal. They too have increased their propensity for counter action against Pretoria. The worldwide focus on apartheid and the debilitating effect on the black populace is growing constantly, along with the internal insurgent movement, international pressures, and the organised campaign within the United Nations to bring about political change.

Currently, the South African Defence Forces are better equipped, thanks partly to Armscor, both to contain any manifestation of resistance within the country and to attack other regional nations providing assistance to the insurgents. Angola and Namibia have provided ideal training grounds for counter-insurgency and conventional operations for the defence establishment. Under P.W. Botha, first as the Defence Minister and then President, defence planning and coordination have been streamlined. The defence forces have been strengthened and enlarged and national support has been demanded of the white community. Armscor has adjusted well to the arms embargoes and has made monumental strides towards self-sufficiency in weapons production. Psychological action programmes, the Civil Defence and local commando infrastructure have been strengthened.

Armscor, now an exporter of weapons systems, is competitive on the world armaments market. Despite temporary setbacks incurred by the 1963 and 1977 arms embargoes, it has increased its state-of-the-art weaponry to such a degree that certain selective weapon

---

*See Appendix B, 'Tracing the Origins of the Arms Embargo', for a comprehensive, yet synoptic historical view of the arms embargo.

systems are considered the best in the world – a good example being, the G6 self-propelled 155 mm gun.

In 1972, the State Security Council was formed to oversee all aspects of the regime's security. The *Defence White Paper*, which P.W. Botha presented to parliament in March 1975, represented the clearest exposition of the thinking of the top ranks of the Defence Force which was the 'Total Strategy' concept. By 1977, the pressure of the Soweto uprisings and the isolation following the Angola invasion gave impetus to a new codified strategic doctrine of the Defence Force spelt out in the Defence White Paper presented to Parliament on 29 March 1977. The White Paper laid out the concept of a unified national security doctrine. Almost every aspect of the State and society was viewed as a legitimate concern of the South African Defence Force. The power of the military in the political arena was further enhanced in August 1979 when P.W. Botha unveiled his Twelve Point Plan integrating the armed forces into the process of administration. Following on the heels of the Plan was the upgrading of the powers of the National Security Management System (NSMS), which was to manage the four power bases (political, economic, social/psychological and security). The pinnacle of the NSMS was the State Security Council (SSC) which today is the focal point of all national decision making.

South Africa has emerged from the 1977 arms embargo as no one's military client. This was emphasised by Chester Crocker, the United States Assistant Secretary of State for African Affairs, on 17 April 1985. However, there are still numerous bodies of evidence that support the effectiveness of the arms embargo against South Africa.

If the arms embargo becomes more stringent, Pretoria will be forced to place more emphasis on manufacture rather than procurement. Both a manufacturing and procurement agency, Armscor now controls arms, ammunition, missile technology, electro-optics, aircraft manufacture and maintenance, pyrotechnic products, armoured vehicles, operational vehicles, vessels, radar and computers, telecommunications, weapons electronics, maritime technology and electronic warfare.

3

Armscor

Armscor has not evolved to its present position as a producer without a large degree of external and internal support spanning over forty years. From South Africa's heavy reliance on the West, particularly Britain and thereafter, France and Israel, to the consolidation of its industrial infrastructure, considerable financing and political support by the government, Armscor has emerged as South Africa's largest exporter of manufactured goods.

As we have already seen, there has been armament production in South Africa since the Second World War. An Advisory Committee on Union Defence Equipment Requirements was appointed in October 1948 to investigate and report on the Union's industrial potential for warlike equipment. In 1949, the Committee became the Defence Resources Board, which existed until 1966.

Lyttleton Engineering Works was previously the Defence Ordnance Workshop which was established in 1953 by the Defence Production Office. Its directive was to provide a stockpile of technical information and manufacturing techniques, and to supply munition requirements. It was replaced by the Armaments Production Board established during 1964 in terms of the Armaments Act, Act No. 87 of 1964.

> During 1968, the Armaments Development and Production Corporation was established with the sole purpose of taking over and managing the two existing factories of the Armaments Production Board and certain strategic facilities owned by private industry.[1]

In referring to the establishment of Armscor, *This is Armscor* states:

> During April 1977, the Armaments Production Board and the old Armscor, amalgamated with a view to controlling the procurement and production of all armaments by one organisation. In this way

the Armaments Corporation of South Africa Ltd. came into being. Armscor's subsidiaries are at present manufacturing a wide range of strategic products varying from aircraft to small-arms ammunition. Private sector industries are requested to produce items ranging from combat vehicles to warships and electronic equipment, and they are also responsible for supplying components and sub-assemblies....[2]

'The U.S. Congress stands guilty of the worst kind of morality – selective morality', said President P.W. Botha, addressing a capacity audience in his first campaign speech in 1987.[3] This, no doubt, is part of the continuum of the readily apparent hard line of Pretoria. Although flexible, but pragmatic, President Botha continues to thrust ahead with that line, not only in his verbal statements but at times, in his not so subtle actions. It seems fitting then that, in order to back his strong rhetoric, the security establishment should continue to be a prominent player in South African events with Armscor playing one of the key roles. With strong support from the State President, Armscor has been able to manufacture locally an impressive array of weapons systems. A credible addition to these new product lines is 'new sonar electronics systems',[4] given the fact that 'the South African Navy (SAN) is not keen to lose its extensive anti-submarine warfare (ASW) experience'.[5] 'The situation is further complicated by the fact that the South African Air Force (SAAF) now no longer has any ASW capability.'[6] Additionally, Armscor announced in July 1983 that design as well as construction of vessels for the South African Navy was in the offing. Armscor previously was involved in the construction phase only, usually with Israeli technical assistance.[7]

On-Line Weapons Systems

On 24 April 1986, the SAS *Drakensburg*, the South African Navy's newest supply ship, was launched. This ship was designed and developed in South Africa. Liebenburg and Stander of Durban carried out the detail and design for the initial 76 million rand project. 'A whole range of locally developed and manufactured systems are built into the SAS *Drakensburg*.'[8] The engineering expertise and logistical support of the shipbuilding industry was now extended to include design. The launching of the *Drakensburg* was the third leg of a triad of weapons systems under the control of Armscor. A month before, the Navy's ninth missile-carrying strike craft, the P1569, had been commissioned and the Alpha XH1 attack helicopter was unveiled soon after. However, despite the Navy's modernisation and self-

PLATE 3.1   Alpha XH1 Tandem Helicopter

sufficiency programme, 'the submarine force is now 15 years old and only the eight 430-ton fast attack craft (missile) can be listed as modern'.[9] Nevertheless, the Navy continues to make strides in the testing of its deadly ship-to-ship Scorpion missiles. In March of 1987, the results of live firing trials, during the naval exercise 'Big Bang', was most impressive. These tests underscored the reliability of the weapons systems of the Durban-built Minister Class strike-craft.[10]

While speaking at the FIDA International Air Show in Santiago, Chile, held from 10–16 March 1986, Mr. Fred Bell, the executive manager of Armscor, in referring to armaments claimed that Armscor remained 'at the forefront of technological development.[11] The Alpha XH1 helicopter attracted the most interest in the show after it had been touted as a major breakthrough in South African aviation technology. If one examines closely the types and relative sophistication of the armaments and previously tested weapons for export by South Africa at the show, a number of conclusions emerge. Casting and special alloys in the aircraft industry are fairly advanced. Guided weapons and optical equipment have a solid grounding in development and production. Artillery and small arms in selected categories approach the state-of-the-art. Heavy-calibre ammunition and bombs are precision assembled. Propellants, rocket motors, rockets and explosives are satisfactory sub-systems for the overall system within which they function. New military equipment on exhibition for export at the show included:

- The sophisticated CB470 system cluster bomb,
- Air-lowered cargo platforms,
- A 120 kg pre-fragmented bomb,
- The GA1 servo-controlled aircraft weapon system, and
- A 20 mm G1 quick-fire cannon.[12]

Private contractors from South Africa such as Sandock-Austral (heavy vehicles), Reutec (shotguns) and Pisa of Durban (parachutes) drew considerable attention from prospective purchasers of security-type equipment. After emphasising the 'impressive list' of weaponry that Armscor is willing to export, the South African Broadcasting Corporation commented, 'It is ironic that it was the weapons boycott that led to South Africa becoming a foremost manufacturer and exporter of arms.'[13]

That list included:

> Several missile systems, including the Cactus and Kukri, a revolutionary helmet sight which enables a fighter pilot to aim at an enemy target merely by looking at it; all 170 types of ammunition required by the

PLATE 3.2   CB470 Cluster Bomb

PLATE 3.3   GA1 Servo-controlled Aircraft Weapon System

PLATE 3.4   20 mm Gi Quick-fire Cannon

PLATE 3.5   Kukri Air-to-Air Missile System

PLATE 3.6   Ratel 60 Command Vehicle

PLATE 3.7   Bosbok Aircraft

Defence Force; the G5 and the mobile G6 155 millimetre field guns – regarded as the best of their kind in the world; Ratel infantry assault vehicles, Samil heavy duty trucks; mine-proof vehicles; Bosbok reconnaissance and Kudu transport planes; several advanced combat rifles and night sights; sophisticated communications equipment, and other defence needs such as coastal strike craft.[14]

South Africa's new helicopter, the Alpha XH1, which is designed to replace the Air Force obsolete French and British machines will give considerable strength to air support capabilities, both internally and in the area of the Namibian border. Of more importance, however, is the knowledge gained in the design and building that can be readily incorporated into other aircraft. This tandem two-seater with the gunner up-front and pilot placed higher and to the rear, is similar in size to the French designed ageing Alouette.

The Atlas Aircraft Corporation built the Alpha XH1 to the following specifications:

Almost directly under the gunner is a 20 mm GA1 servo-controlled cannon aimed by a helmet-mounted sight. This can fire at the rate of 600 rounds a minute, through an elevation of from plus-10 to minus-10 degrees. The aircraft has a maximum take-off mass of 2,200 kilogrammes and is powered by a single gas-turbine engine.[15]

PLATE 3.8   Kudu Aircraft

PLATE 3.9   BXP Sub-machine Gun

After 12 years of intense research, Dr. Maitland Reed, a Durban aviation engineer, designed an advanced pilotless aircraft (drone), the Eyrie, which will be marketed by Armscor. However, the new milestone for the Air Force is the upgrading the Mirage III fighter into the Cheetah by the Atlas Aircraft Corporation, a subsidiary of the Armaments Corporation of South Africa. Nearly 50 per cent of the Mirage III has been reconstructed and equipped with the latest navigational equipment and weapons. This cost-efficient method for obtaining 'new aircraft' was praised by both the State President and the leaders of the armaments industry. These three dramatic breakthroughs, the Cheetah, Alpha XH1 and the Eyrie, have been well publicized and have enhanced the morale of the members of Armscor and its subsidiaries. The Defence Force's policy of 'planned evolution' was underscored by a statement on 16 July 1986 by the Minister of Defence, General Magnus Malan, 'With the launch of the Cheetah aircraft we are entering a new era of self-sufficiency and an enhanced operational capability. ...'[16] An underlying reason for the concentration of efforts on the Cheetah was the inevitable concern felt over the capability of the Soviet-made MiG-23 aircraft and ground weaponry in Angola. Mr. Don Kerr, an aircraft expert from Britain, brought this out in his pointed statement:

PLATE 3.10   Cheetah Fighter Aircraft

PLATE 3.11   Mirage III Fighter Aircraft

> I am sure it is more than a match for the MiG-23s in Angola. I suspect that Armscor with the SAAF has given the Mirage a ground attack capability and it has involved their usual very high standard of ingenuity and feet-on-the-ground engineering.[17]

The *Beeld*, known for its 'no frills' comments, had this to say on the Cheetah.

> It is rather ironic but also significant that an advanced and highly sophisticated piece of weaponry could be added to South Africa's already formidable armoury at a time when the sanctions chorus was shouting at its loudest.
> To a venomous world this latest breakthrough is, on the one hand, proof that South Africa will not let itself be bullied and, on the other, an admonition to those who naively maintain that effective sanctions can be carried out.[18]

There are no new big ticket items being manufactured for the ground forces but considerable research and development money is being spent on anti-tank weapons, including anti-tank guided weapons. South Africa is disinclined to develop a battle tank.[19] The French Panhard armoured car was re-adapted for bush warfare by Armscor and is known as the Eland. This highly versatile, heavily armed vehicle

PLATE 3.12   Ratel 90 APC

has been exported as 'combat' tested in Namibia and Angola. The
refit programme was considerably less sophisticated in terms of design
and engineering than, for example, the rehabilitation of the Mirage
into the Cheetah. The relatively new Ingwe (Leopard) vehicle was
designed by Sandock-Austral specifically for organisations that have
a need for protective security like mining industries, certain agencies
and municipalities. Knowledge and design for the Ingwe were drawn
from existing knowledge of the Eland armoured car and the Ratel
armoured personnel carrier. The Ingwe is a 'versatile vehicle with
variants which find application with a wide range of users – from
civilian security companies through police to military applications'.[20]
It uses proven commercially available components such as the locally
produced Atlantic kw 123 diesel engine, gearbox and axles. By July
1986, the total production had been sold, which attests to the
dependability and versatility of this vehicle.

   A proven armoured personnel carrier, the Casspir, has unmatched
levels of protection and mobility and is now available for sale to a
wide variety of para-military and military organisations. This vehicle
is well-suited for riot control conditions and comes with a wide-array
of specialised options like flood and searchlights, sirens, rubber bullet
launchers, pneumatically controlled drop-down road clearing obstacle

bumpers, protected windows, spherical gun mountings in the windshield, etc. It is also designed to suffer only superficial damage from the most common types of anti-tank mine (notable the TM57 variety).

On 22 October 1988, Armscor unveiled its new armoured vehicle, the Rooikat. This eight-wheeled, Panzer-like vehicle is unique. Its stabilised turret permits rapid fire from its 76 mm computer-assisted gun while traversing rough terrain, hitting tanks at a range of 1.25 miles. The Rooikat went into production in early 1989 and will be operational in the South African Army by late 1989. Its operating range is 620 miles at speeds of 75 miles per hour on paved roads and 37 miles per hour cross country. Its eight-wheel drive powers it to gradients of 70 per cent.

There has also been a concerted move by Armscor to improve communications equipment to be used in a combat environment. Thus, the development of the backpack portable message centre, Grinel's (Grinaker Electronics (Pty.) Ltd.) personal communications centre with state-of-the-art ECCM. This frequency-hopping radio marks a giant step forward for troops on the ground.

The 'Joint Arms Industry'

Through the so-called 'joint arms industry',[21] South Africa and Israel have developed what is supposedly an armour plating for tanks as the most effective in the world. The open secret of the Israeli-South African joint ventures has not diminished the *modus operandi* of either country. The genesis of the 'joint arms industry' may be found in Prime Minister John Vorster's visit to Israel in April 1976. A multitude of events then unfolded, some of which paint a more vivid picture within the open secret:

- Reshef missile boats and Dabur patrol boats, fitted with Gabriel ship-to-ship missiles to Pretoria. (Gabriel is known as Skorpion in South Africa.)
- Night vision equipment for helicopters to Pretoria.
- Active Israeli servicemen on secondment to South Africa.
- Co-operation in defence interests.
- Agreements on the establishment of an electronics industry in South Africa.
- Electronic and infra-red border-sensing equipment and electronic border fence to South Africa.
- The arms connection with South Africa created 5,000 jobs in Israel.[22]

- South Africa's rare minerals in trade for Israeli know-how.
- Possible LAVI aircraft connection in the form of engineering, avionics and airframe blueprints.
- Possible spin-off to South Africa of the joint United States-Israeli submarine building project.

Though Armscor can stand alone on some armaments, it must be realised that the Israeli connection has been largely responsible for enabling Pretoria to take short cuts in producing weapons systems and related products. The Israeli designed UZI machine gun, a copy of the Galil assault rifle and R4 are produced in South Africa. Israeli technology is behind the Minister strike craft patrol boats, the Skorpion surface-to-surface missiles and the tank retrofitting programme. Within this technology that the Israelis have given to Armscor, the most important is in the field of electronics. With Israeli know-how and Armscor's almost total self-sufficiency in the production of ferro-alloys, high grade steels plus non-ferrous metals, they have made an unbeatable team in arms production.

A Secret United States Report

The sanctions law enacted by the United States Congress over President Reagan's veto recommends that aid be rescinded for those nations selling arms and military technology to South Africa.

PLATE 3.13   Oliphant Tank Retriever

Furthermore, the law calls for the State Department to submit a report to Congress detailing the technology and arms of nations who are circumventing the mandatory arms embargo of 1977. This secret report was sent to Congress on 1 April 1987. Only a short, sanitised version is open to public scrutiny. Britain, France, West Germany, Italy, Switzerland, and Israel were named as suppliers to South Africa. In response to this report, French Premier Jacques Chirac said, 'May I tell you that France stopped the sale of armaments to South Africa about 10 years ago.'[23] Of course, this is technically true since armaments sold to South Africa have been through independent manufacturers, not the French Government. However, this is not true in the case of Israel in which the state owns and controls all armament manufacture and sale. Within this context it is important to note that in anticipation of the damning allegations in the report, Israel's Prime Minister Shimon Peres openly acknowledged the close military association with Pretoria on 19 March 1987.

As a sidelight, one should be aware of the self-serving need of political expediency and pragmatism of American politicians. The phraseology of 'recommending' that President Reagan 'consider' cutting off military aid to those not conforming to the sanctions law, was a compromise. In that context, the following is germane:

> Sen. Alan Cranston, the California Democrat who is a leading proponent of the sanctions, voted against the report's provision last year when the matter arose in the Senate Foreign Relations Committee.
>
> Mr. Cranston's new trade embargo bill, which is identical in every other way to one offered in the House by Representative Ronald Dellums, California Democrat, omits the foreign aid cut-off to nations that sell weaponry or military technology to South Africa ....
>
> Mr. Cranston received $125,000 from January through July of 1986 from Israeli political action committees (PACs), according to the Federal Elections Commission. That amount was the second highest total any lawmaker received from American–Israel PACs during the same period.[24]

The report generated considerable pointed comment from various circles. Faris Bouhafa, a spokesman for the American-Arab Anti-Discrimination Committee, said the report 'is going to put a number of lawmakers on the hill in a difficult position because, historically, there has been very little inclination to hold Israel to the same standards of international behaviour advocated for other countries who have relationships with the United States'.[25]

The State Department said that information in the report was not more detailed because the majority of arms sales are secret and, 'As a result, we have a partial, incomplete and somewhat random picture.'[26] John M. Goshko of the Washington Post had this to say about it:

> The report states that defence companies in France, Italy and Israel – probably with the knowledge of their governments – have helped maintain and upgrade major weapons systems provided to South Africa before the United Nations approved an embargo on such weapons sales in 1977. It also said weapons firms in West Germany, Britain, Switzerland and the Netherlands have violated the embargo 'on occasion', either without government approval or 'in the gray area between civilian and military applications ...' Senate Foreign Relations Comittee Chairman Pell (D-RI) said, 'The report already has had a positive impact' on Israel.[27]

There is little indication that Israel has modified its South African connection despite claims to the contrary. All indications point to a business-as-usual approach between Pretoria and Tel Aviv. This approach, however, is currently less open.

PLATE 3.14   G6 155 mm Howitzers

PLATE 3.15   Pretoria Metal Pressings Plant

PLATE 3.16   Swartklip Products

PLATE 3.17   Ratel Logistics Vehicle

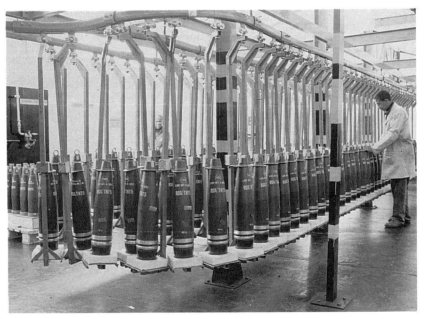

PLATE 3.18   Naschem Ammunition Plant

The 'Magic Eleven'

Even though 1,000 private contractors account for over 70 per cent of the armaments manufactured and supplied to the South African Defence Force, Armscor has a number of servicing subsidiaries, ten manufacturing subsidiaries and its most recent accession, a weapons systems Research Laboratory. These 'magic eleven' are shown below and have the responsibilities indicated:

Company	Location
ATLAS AIRCRAFT CORPORATION TELCAST Aircraft manufacture, maintenance and service. High technology with special alloys.	KEMPTON PARK
INFOPLAN Computer services	PRETORIA
KENTRON Design and manufacture of guided-weapons systems	PRETORIA
ELOPTRO Manufacture of optical, electro-optical equipment	KEMPTON PARK
LYTTLETON ENGINEERING WORKS (LEW) Manufacture of small arms, mortars and cannons.	VERWOERDBURG
MUSGRAVE MANUFACTURERS AND DISTRIBUTORS Manufacture and marketing of commercial rifles, shotguns and handguns	BLOEMFONTEIN
NASHEM Filling of mortar and aircraft bombs, heavy calibre ammunition and mines	LENZ* AND POTCHEFSTROOM
PRETORIA METAL PRESSINGS (PMP) Manufacture of small-calibre and quick-fire ammunition	PRETORIA WEST
SOMCHEM Manufacture of propellants, explosives, rocket-propulsion systems and rockets	SOMERSET WEST AND WELLINGTON
SWARTKLIP PRODUCTS Manufacture of pyrotechnical products, hand-grenades and commercial ammunitions	CAPE FLATS
HOUWTEG (PTY.) LTD Think-tank, linked to missile-testing range at De Hoop on the Bredasdrop coast[28]	HOUWHOEK, CAPE

Sources of South Africa's Internal Strength

Armscor's position of strength within the power structure of the South African Government emanates from various and varied sources. These

*The Lenz Explosive Manufacturing plant is due to be phased out by March 1989.

PLATE 3.19   Pretoria Metal Pressings

sources, like spokes on a wheel, give Armscor considerable leverage within the government, industry and the economy. B. A. Cox and C. M. Rogerson investigated the network and geographical fabric of interlocking directorates in South Africa. They came to the conclusion that corporate power in South Africa is dominated by a small elite group which has its power through tightly knit connections of interlocking directorships. 'The weave of cross-directorships, which revolves around these large enterprises, points to a conclusion that the majority of leading South African companies are drawn into what appears to be *one* national network of interlocked directorships.'[29] This no doubt applies to Armscor as well as companies with even larger assets such as Anglo-American, Barlows, Volkskas, Nedbank and others. Cox and Rogerson go on to say, 'The only enterprises which appear to be "independent" of this national network of interlocked directorships are run either by maverick industrial entre-preneurs or those with strong "ethnic" ties. Illustratively ... are companies drawn almost entirely from the Jewish community. ...'[30] The weight of corporate control has its centre in Johannesburg which dominates the sectors of banking, financing, industry, retailing and real estate. 'Almost two-thirds of the assets of 100 South African industrial concerns were controlled from Johannesburg. ...'[31]

Armscor's new head office which now consolidates activities that were previously spread over 15 sites and buildings in the Pretoria/ Johannesburg area is part of those enterprises that share in 'the weave of cross-directorships'.

Secondly, the State Security Council (SSC), where security policy is determined and its co-ordinated implementation is delegated downward, becomes a crucial body in Armscor's schema for budget generation and influential movement within the political structure. State President Botha, former Minister of Defence and a strong advocate in the propagation of the themes 'total national strategy*' and 'total onslaught', obviously, is the key player in determining security considerations. Of the four cabinet committees, the SSC is by far the most influential because of its structure and support personnel. 'The SSC has a complex of supporting agencies and committees more extensive and complete than any other cabinet committee.'[32] There have been accusations that the SSC was indeed shaping government policy. Because it is empowered to make decisions, it looms as an ominous body in the decision-making process within the State.

The full membership of the SSC is not disclosed. However, primary members like the State President, Ministers of Defence, Foreign Affairs, Law and Order, and Justice are established by law. On the other hand, 'others' who are given 'primary' status are not so named in law. Also, certain professionals and top-ranking civil servants are included in the Council. The point to be made here is that certain key and influential members of the SSC are not directly responsible to Parliament. When weapons development and armaments are discussed, the Chairman of Armscor most probably attends. The power of the SSC has seen a marked upswing over the years. This had its genesis in the 1975 investigational report that recommended an active security management system to link all agencies into a security network. Grundy points out that 'SADF officers are prominent in all high-level interdepartmental committees of the SSC ... they do illustrate the ubiquity of such security ties and their potential for influence.'[33]

Thirdly, the strength of the Defence Force cannot be denied,

---

*In 1978, P.W. Botha shifted the emphasis of a regional policy to 'total strategy'. The objective was to create a 'constellation of states' that included the 'independent' Bantustans in addition to the states of Botswana, Swaziland, Lesotho, Zimbabwe and Namibia.

These states were to be included in a co-operative politico-military-economic order having the nexus centred on the internally 'reformed' South Africa.

despite spokesmen for the defence establishment continually wanting increased appropriations and manpower because of the ever-present threat (in this case 'total onslaught'). The South African Defence Force is the strongest and *most able* in Africa. Thus, through its economic and political strength, it uses its power to obtain weapons systems, thereby subsidising an influential organisation such as Armscor.

Fourthly, the paranoia behind the arms embargo has generated an inner *laager* within the existing *laager* mentality of Pretoria. The 'go-it-alone' policy, if all else fails, has given Armscor the additional momentum to manufacture weapons rather than procure them.

Fifth, the defence budget is still within very acceptable limits as a percentage of GNP. The Defence budget for financial year 1986/87 represented the lowest percentage of GNP (3.5 per cent) since 1980/81 (3.1 per cent). The highest, 4.9 per cent, was in 1976/77. This obviously gives room for manoeuvre by the proponents of a stronger Defence Force of which, of course, the vested interest of Armscor looms largest. (See Appendix A for 1987/88 South African Defence Budget.)

Sixth, Botha and his 'total strategy' and 'total onslaught' continually generates considerable awareness among both the hardliner and the moderate white population. Their overall perceptions of the threat have been such that they have avoided any vigorous challenge of defence expenditure. This type of political defence strategy of Pretoria is not unlike the United States Pentagon's strategy of first, creating an awareness, then cultivating the public's perception, and secondly, playing up to and on this 'cultivated perception' so the majority of the populace becomes almost frenzied by the looming 'bogeyman'. In the case of the United States, that 'bogeyman' is the Soviet Union. In the case of South Africa, however, it is both the external threat of the Soviet Union and the internal threat of communist agitators.

Thus, we see the six sources of internal South African strength for Armscor: interlocking directorates, the State Security Council, the South African Defence Force, the spin-off of the arms embargo, the defence budget and P.W. Botha's carefully calculated cultivation of public perception, and how they place the armaments industry in a power-broker position.

4

The Web of Arms Procurement

Even though Armscor maintains a relatively strong position within the corporate and governmental structures, the domestic scene is such that a continuation of the overall economic downward slide may very well have an eroding effect on the strength of its position. The multilaterally applied international sanctions, threats of private boycotts, the debt, and the international banking community's policy towards re-loaning money to South Africa, has a dampening impact on the growth of the economy. South Africa has had to generate its own capital requirements while continuing to be a capital exporter. One must be aware that the arms embargo has had the short term effect of generating growth in the arms industry through import substitution. 'In the longer term, however, if we assume a situation of co-ordinated, punitive and ratcheting sanctions, the growth of the economy, undoubtedly, will be adversely affected, i.e. increasing international isolation will put South Africa squarely on to a low growth path.'[1]

If this turns out to be true, there will be strong competition for the budget dollar in which case, the Minister of Defence will need to sell its case with additional panache and skill. According to Johan C. van Zyl, '... the key to rejuvenated economic growth in South Africa is effective political accommodation of blacks.'[2] This, of course, will most likely involve forms of violence on either side, perhaps a 'violent stalemate', in which the time will not be ripe for a prevailing democratic solution in the near future. But, on the other hand, if all forces seek a genuine compromise solution, not from an altruistic spirit but from pragmatic necessity borne from the perception of the need for survival, then something short of a democratic solution has a very good chance of emerging. As Van Zyl points out, the outcome could be regional power-sharing along the line of the Indaba movement in Natal province. The platform comprises political compromise, increasing devolution of power and a private enterprise-oriented social market economy.[3] These 'ifs' could have a profound effectual change on the role of Armscor.

On the other hand, South Africa is at a crossroads where there are basically three ways to go – Right, Left or Centre. The way of the Conservative Party (Right) centres on partition. Africa being a winner-take-all continent, there is no room for the middle ground. Power sharing would inevitably lead to the domination of whites by blacks. Therefore, in Pretoria's eyes, the only way to arrest this forgone conclusion is to divide the land. Each group would have sovereignty over its own affairs. This philosophy is given considerable credence by certain whites as they are exposed to a declining economic situation, rising risks to their security and a view that support systems are declining.

At the other end of this spectrum are the blacks on the left. Revolution appears extremely attractive to those who have been excluded from the mainstream of society and have absolutely no say in their own affairs. Their view is that revolution has a rational basis.

In the centre of these two opposing poles are moderate whites and blacks. But, declining economic growth has a tendency to withdraw white support from the centre to more right wing movements. Declining growth also fuels the fire of revolution due to increasingly limited options for those blacks who had minimal manoeuvring room to start with. However, what is essential is that a clear and distinct alternative must evolve in the place either of partition or of a pure socialist state. Both subsume the needs of the individual to the goals of the state. Therefore, the individual becomes subjugated not elevated. Besides a concentration on the sanctity of the individual, negotiations must at all times take priority over armed conflict. Superimposed on a high regard for individual rights and for negotiations must be a decent standard of living for all. Only by creating new wealth and having this wealth touch all segments of society will the forces of change be meaningful and therefore lasting. It is not unreasonable to expect South Africa's per capita income to double by the year 2000. All that would be required is a growth rate of 8 per cent per annum. An integrated economy would be futile under the patchwork system of nation-states with competing sovereignties such as the partition group seeks. Ostensibly, a full-blown socialist system has failed to make sizeable inroads into economic growth anywhere in the world.

All three conditions, sanctity of the individual, negotiations, and a decent standard of living, have to be filled simultaneously. South Africa can no longer afford large bodies within the populace to be alienated.*

With the above scenarios in mind, Armscor would have a role to play albeit different within each scenario. The Conservative Party's partition scenario will not necessarily enhance the growth of Armscor but will most likely entail a more inward-looking armaments industry. A distinct and separate white flotilla navigating within black waters will inevitably create a smaller and more inclusive *laager* bent on maintaining a 'purity' that will be the antithesis of moving toward membership in the international community. The result will be isolation and internal xenophobic response to the world around them. However, if the partitioners desire to maintain Armscor's position as the top manufacturing exporter they may have to make certain social and economic adjustments that would effect whites only. Heretofore, the entire state of South Africa was the 'monopoly board' for social and economic engineering, invariably affecting blacks much less advantageously than whites. Land acquisition for testing sites and airfields, access to black labour pools, and maintaining highly trained technical specialists in such an inwardly-looking society would be difficult at best. Economic flexibility would be considerably less than in present day South Africa.

The pure socialist state would entail a high probability that Armscor's role as we know it today would change considerably. If the government leaned toward the Soviet bloc there would be no need for internal arms production. The Soviets would be glad to supply arms to increase its influence over its client. Furthermore, the infrastructure of Armscor would have eroded considerably with the knowledge that a pure socialist state was in the offing. The so-called 'chicken run' of highly-skilled workers, seeking employment elsewhere, would start long before the new government took office. In the unlikely event that the pure socialist state desired to be no one's client, realising the revenue-generating potential of Armscor and desired to maintain a modern military force, an accommodation could be reached. However, this accommodation would be complex. Because

---

*'The 3 ways to go', partition, pure socialist state, moderate position are treated in Clem Sunter's 'Trump Cards', the *High Road*, a Leadership Publication, April 1988, pp. 87/88.
The above analysis has its genesis in Sunter's work.

of Armscor's unique work force and technological base, it would have to be granted special status that would smack of elitism. If the State's pragmatism overrode its ideology, one might see this scenario unfolding. However, that scenario is less probable because the leadership of Armscor is too entrenched in Afrikanerdom.

The moderate position ensures an Armscor not too different from today – a supplier of internal armaments and an international arms exporter. However, indications would point to less of a need for internal markets and more concentration on research and development directed toward the export market. If the economy grows substantially and internal dissension diminishes, the need for counter-insurgency armaments decreases. But, under the moderate approach, international pressures caused heretofore by the 'apartheid regime' would be considerably lessened. This, in its turn, would be a plus in international trade for South Africa. Armscor would benefit from this.

The moderate approach is rapidly being given more credence, although no one is foolish enough to provide a timetable. Racial exclusiveness and white-power dominance have been written off. The national point of discussion has changed from white dominance to white security; from white leadership to white participation in future systems; from systematic exclusion to societal amalgamation. A revolutionary type of thinking is taking place. Viewed from any perspective, the same answer floats to the top. The critical aspect of South African politics, in the near term, is not the accommodation of blacks, but accommodation of whites. However, in the light of the stronger probability that business will continue as usual in the near future, Armscor should maintain its viability as a player within the economic and political structure of South Africa.

The Board of Directors of Armscor consists of seven to twelve members. The ex-officio member is the head of the South African Defence Force. All other members, including the Chairman, are appointed by the State President. The beginning of the evolution for a weapons system starts with the Defence Force defining a requirement based on an assessment of the threat and/or a need to fulfil any void created by future strategy and tactics. The guidelines for the provision of armaments is laid out in the document *Policy and Procedure for the Procurement of Material*. The requirement phase could turn out to be a 'grab bag' in which the Defence Force could come up with a 'pig in a poke' if it weren't for the technical advice of Armscor who definitively assesses the system, arriving at a clear and accurate portrayal of the weapons system based upon the Defence Force's stated requirement. A project team, consisting of members of the Defence Force and Armscor, is formed. Like any project study, solutions are identified. Those that are practical are analysed until the system in question meets the demands of the previously determined and specified requirement. Complex solutions require a development phase of the entire technical design, and, if applicable, a working prototype. The incentive for firm control of the cost of the design and prototype is the contractual arrangement whereby, in most cases, the production of the system goes to that Armscor subsidiary or private contractor who developed the most satisfactory prototype.

Inner Workings

The evaluation of the prototype trials results, during the procurement study, is the largest step in the aquisition of valuable use data, production costs and manufacturing milestones. The bottom line, however, is that the procurement study fine tunes the cost estimate, including the cost of the logistical support tail. This, no doubt, is critical. After Defence Force approval, Armscor enters into a contractual arrangement with the designated subsidiary or private contractor. Armscor's function during manufacture is to ensure quality control and that all specifications are met. Depending upon the contract, the manufacturer's most pressing concerns are cost and time. Affecting these are price escalation, rate-of-exchange adjustments, user documentation and training. Armscor provides considerable guidance and expertise in these areas.

It becomes incumbent upon Armscor to utilise the private sector to the full. As one of its major responsibilities, Armscor's organisational structure is geared for this particular task. Management functions are structured in such a way as to provide flexibility whilst at the same time providing the in-depth overseer capabilities which play so necessary a part in the comprehensive coordination required for today's sophisticated weapons systems.

It becomes readily apparent that the need for in-house manufacturing must be balanced against the outside procurement process. Procurement is viewed in the context of trade-offs – is the system better, less costly? Does it produce a reliable supplier and licencing guarantees if the suppliers default, and so on? Always at the forefront of decision making on armaments is standardisation. The lower the level to which standardisation is achieved, the greater the flexibility and cost effectiveness of the project. For example, the standardisation of sub-assemblies and components is good, but interchangeable parts within components and sub-assemblies would be better.

Part of Armscor's long-range goal is that the capabilities, technological expertise and know-how will pay dividends for the industrial sector through South Africa's arms export programme. The range of arms and armaments, both for internal consumption and export, has been covered previously. These weapons systems and auxiliary equipment compare favourably in quality with the best in the world. This says a great deal about the quality-assurance mechanism of Armscor.

Like any large successful organisation, Armscor places considerable emphasis on personnel management. Salaries compare with the private sector and fringe benefits are above the norm. At any one time there are approximately 5,000 employees undergoing various types of training. Tuition grants are provided to university students in selected fields. These grants do not require the students to work for Armscor after graduation. However, three-quarters of the students do so. The combination of pay, morale, sense of accomplishment, fulfilment, working conditions and a sense of contribution are all part of the ongoing effort of Armscor's 'people programme' to ensure a happy and productive work force.

Although Armscor can be considered an autonomous corporation, it does receive financial support from the government as well as from private banking institutions. Its share capital and reserve funds are in excess of R700 million and it procures armaments in excess of R1,500 million annually. Company assets are over R2.8 billion. Armscor has become the largest single exporter of manufactured goods in South Africa, with sales to foreign countries valued in 1987 at R1.8 billion. Their budget allocation for 1987/88 was R3 billion.

Generally speaking, in the past Armscor tended to keep its infrastructure functioning through foreign licences. Now the policy is a more direct sales approach. The question then arises, where is Armscor heading and how does it intend to get there?

Capacity, Research and Development

It is difficult to arrive at a definitive percentage of the manufacturing capacity currently being used. However, facilities are running at between 70 and 100 per cent. Products are normally divided into durables and expendables. Ammunition, an expendable, must be replaced immediately, whereas weapons systems, being durables, have continued use, barring maintenance problems or destruction. The replacement of main weapons systems requires a continuous manufacturing and production run. Ammunition replacement production, on the other hand, can be erratic. It is generally felt throughout Defence that the SADF should not find itself in the position it was in in 1965 or 1970. Weapons systems were antiquated and the majority of arms were Second World War vintage. 'Once bitten, twice shy', said Commandant Piet Marais, Chairman of Armscor.* A matter for concern is what technologically advanced weapons the Soviets are supplying to other African countries. A sophisticated South African intelligence network feeds this information to the Ministry of Defence, which, through Armscor, maintains a substantial research and development (R&D) programme staffed with the best available minds. All this is directed toward the 'Threat'. The arms embargo has necessitated the heavy thrust into R&D. Anyone looking closely at the intense efforts put into the development of the 'Cheetah' fighter aircraft due to go into full-scale production in the 1990s, could easily surmise that it was designed primarily to counter Zimbabwe's twelve recently purchased MiG-29s to be delivered in mid-1989. Most aviation experts have praised the capability of the Cheetah over Angola's MiG-23s. However, a strong case can also be made to show that South African intelligence was keenly aware of the pending Zimbabwe-Soviet MiG-29 deal, well in advance of the April 1987 newsbreak.[4] Although the standard Soviet MiG-29 would appear to be superior to the Cheetah, this will probably not be the case, due to some very important overriding factors. First of all, Zimbabwe will most likely receive the export version, i.e. without the sophisticated avionics; secondly, the range of the MiG-29 is 500 miles where the Cheetah's is 750 miles.[5] Since Zimbabwe has no inflight refuelling capability the MiG-29s will more than likely be used only in a defensive role.†

The R&D effort put into the G6 155 mm artillery system represented a major achievement. The G6 was the outcome of the SADF being outgunned in the Angolan war. In 1975 the old 5.5 inch artillery pieces (range, 17 kilometres) were relatively ineffective. The army needed a gun that had a greater range than the 26 kilometres of the

---

*He was referring to the Soviets. In 1974, in Angola, the South African forces had almost reached Luanda when they suddenly, and unexpectedly, found their artillery was being outranged by weapons supplied by the Soviet Union.

†An officer in the South African Air Force, said to me, 'The rooster now has a beautiful array of peacock feathers but Ivan has clipped the rooster's spurs.'

Soviet artillery being used in Angola. Thus, the cycle was initiated – the Army laid down the requirement, based on the perceived hostile threat. Armscor then completed the cycle. There were two ways to go. Buy a system on the open market, with all the complications that the upcoming mandatory arms embargo would entail, or manufacture an artillery system in-house. The latter was chosen. From the concept for extended range artillery, which was highly theoretical, to the prototype barrels, to testing, to assemblage with many trial and error periods along the way, the G5 155 mm was born (the G6 155 mm is self-propelled).

Problems on the path to success were legion. Lacking the computing capability to test the theoretical framework, Armscor employed a company called SRC in Canada, headed by Gerry Bull, a dual-nationality American-Canadian citizen. Bull, who was working on some of his own concepts for long-range artillery, ran Armscor's theoretical calculations on his computers. Financial difficulty and Bull's conviction for contravening the United Nations' arms embargo, were ironic events that led to Armscor buying shares in SRC and, in a sub-rosa manoeuvre, placing key management personnel in the firm. Prototype barrels and projectiles were tested through a joint consortium of Bull's and Armscor's engineers on the island of Antigua. The tests were fruitful. The tested prototypes were shipped to South Africa and, from 1976 onwards, Armscor developed the artillery system. After numerous tests, the G5 was redesigned into a viable artillery weapons system. Because of various agreements and licencing arrangements, Gerry Bull, after he went bankrupt, sold the design of the gun to Voest Alpine in Austria. In the meantime, Armscor continued to upgrade this artillery system with muzzle velocity radar and other sophisticated improvements. The next mark in this series, the G6, was entirely a South African design.

Tailoring Weapons Systems

It seems that South Africa tailors its weapons needs to the environment better than any other African country. One need only consider the 1987 March/April Libyan/Chad conflict to see that sophisticated weapons systems can become a liability in certain environments. Toyota trucks with mounted machine guns and hand-held rocket launchers defeated an armada of Soviet-built tanks. On the other hand, the November 1987 military success of Jonas Savimbi's UNITA Forces against Angola's Soviet directed FAPLA forces was in no

PLATE 4.1   G5 155 mm Howitzers (towed)

small part due to the sophisticated SADF-operated weapons employed against Angola. Armscor's highly-touted and sophisticated artillery pieces (notably the G5 and the self-propelled G6)* were applied with deadly efficiency at critical stages of the conflict. This, no doubt, will give additonal credibility to Armscor's extensive advertising campaign, 'Field Tested in Combat'.

The South African Defence Force does a credible job of creating the right mix between environment, tactics and weapons systems. For instance, the operational areas of Namibia and Southern Angola include enormous distances. Penetrations of forces beyond 300 kilometres is not uncommon. Speed, manoeuvre, night movement and shock action become critical in this type of bush country. Daylight movement is out of the question because of Soviet satellites. The Eland is a superior mobile weapons system with a 1,000 kilometre range, good speed, and it functions well during periods of reduced

---

*South Africa had used up to seventy of its G6 gun-howitzers around the Lomba river in Angola. More than 14 per cent of the 25,000 FAPLA troops died and an estimated 10,000 were wounded – an estimated 54 per cent loss. *Jane's Defence Weekly* estimated FAPLA's loss at R2,000 million. This would be one half of the reported R4,000 million the Soviets have sent to Angola in the past four years. – As reported in the *Star*, 29 Nov. 87, P8.

PLATE 4.2   G6 155 mm Howitzer (SP)

PLATE 4.3   Ratel 12.7 mm APCS

visibility. The tanks that the South Africans do possess are not suitable for this type of warfare. Nevertheless, they are an important part of the weapons inventory in case of a conventional conflict in which armoured battles are likely to be fought. On the other hand, South Africa's G6 155 mm self-propelled gun-howitzer is a prime example of engineering and user input. It has the distinction of being the only wheeled self-propelled artillery weapons system outside the Warsaw Pact. The G6 is likely to operate some distance from main bases, perhaps up to 1,000 kilometres. Tracked vehicles are much noisier, break down more frequently and consume more fuel. The G6 lessens the logistic requirement in the Southern African area. The point to be made is that the South African Defence Force's well thought out tactical solutions are based on numerous inputs, not the least of which is the environment. In many military circles the belief is still that the best defence against a tank is another tank. However, this line of thought may become less tenable in the light of the R&D being performed on technologically sophisticated anti-tank missile systems. Armscor has made quite good progress with the R&D of anti-tank guided weapons. Piet Marais has admitted, 'We are spending a lot of R&D money on anti-tank weapons in general.'[6]

In 1984, the research staff of the South African Institute of Race

PLATE 4.4   Ratel 90 APC

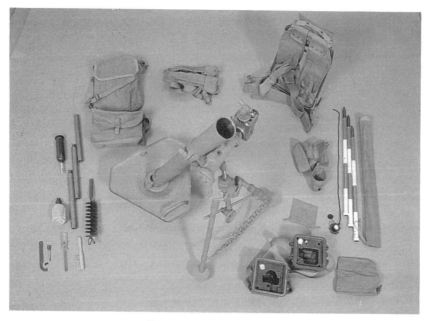

PLATE 4.5   60 mm Mortar

PLATE 4.6   120 mm Mortar

Relations from Johannesburg stated, 'There was also an immediate shortage of attack helicopters but little chance of a helicopter being produced by Armscor in the immediate future'[7] This prediction was obviously proved wrong by the intensive R&D efforts that led to the unveiling of the Alpha XH1 helicopter in April 1986.

R&D is realised by Armscor as the inchoation of the manufacture of state-of-the-art weaponry. Therefore, additional emphasis is being placed on this initial stage in the cycle for producing armaments. If one looks at the Defence Force's recent 1.4 million item computerised codification programme and the new medium speed wind tunnel designed for aircraft aerodynamics research, the R&D effort certainly can not be looked upon as a modicum of the defence budget. In referring to the codification programme, *The Citizen* said, '... which could save the country and private enterprise, billions of rands ... Computerised data would make it possible for more rational storing of parts ... accessibility ... availability ...'[8] In commenting on the wind tunnel, *Pretoria News* reported a wealth of information on the inter-relationships of R&D, private industry, external sources and the government:

> Aircraft aerodynamics research in South Africa took a major step forward on January 15 with the delivery of a new medium-speed wind tunnel to the Council for Scientific and Industrial Research's (CSIR) National Institute for Aeronautics and Systems Technology in Pretoria. The new wind tunnel is part of a R60 million project. Designed in America, it weighs over 140 tons and was built in South Africa. The huge wind tunnel was delivered to the CSIR's site by two giant trucks and was one of the heaviest loads yet delivered by road in South Africa.[9]

One has merely to follow the leading international defence journals to keep abreast of the growing R&D effort of Armscor. A major boost to Armscor's research facilities is a new site near Cape Town. The 15,000 square metre weapons systems research laboratory, set on a 505 hectare site, is at Houwhoek, near Cape Town. The company has set up a new subsidiary company called Houwteg, which is expected eventually to employ some 400 people – 90 per cent of them engineers and scientists who will work on missiles and other advanced systems. The site of the R&D laboratory is conveniently located for access to Armscor's missile range at De Hoop near Bredasdorp.

Prevailing Mood

As one analyses the statements of opinion makers and government officials in South Africa from 1985 through 1987, a definite mood

prevails within the 'misunderstood *Afrikaner*', who has overcome one
internationally generated adversity after another. Under this pressure
they have gained a perceptual strength that has reached an almost
euphoric high, based on a philosophy that 'we have *laagered* against
the world and we are winning – indeed we must be a chosen people'.
The reasoning goes, after all, 'look at what Israel has accomplished
in the face of insurmountable odds.' Pretoria's association with Israel
goes well beyond the symbiotic relationship established in terms of
military and nuclear collaboration in the 1960s. A kind of mimicry
of Israeli *modus operandi* is prevalent among the ruling élite of South
Africa. Both Israel and the RSA see themselves as 'Westernized'. A
commonality of fate acts as a magnet in their relationship. After all,
the United Nations equated Zionism with racism and *apartheid. The
Economist* said that the ideal ally for Israel shoud possess the following:

> Ideally, such an ally should not be susceptible to American influence;
> should have shared geopolitical interests with Israel, and above all,
> should have the resources and technology needed to help build a
> sophisticated weapons industry.[10]

Both nations have adopted a strategy for survival. In nuclear
development and military co-operation, Israel is South Africa's only
overt partner. Both are essentially white, Europeanised peoples who
view their countries as being surrounded by hostile forces of non-
European majorities. Israel's victory over the Arabs in 1967 has
become a blueprint for Pretoria's armaments industry. Technology,
superior weapons and tactical employment were the key to Israeli
success. This same road is being taken by South Africa. The South
Africans have modelled themselves in the Israeli mode. One can
defend oneself against terrorists and liberation movements in a hostile
environment if one possesses the will and sophisticated armaments
necessary to defeat and thwart countermoves of the opposition with
technology, sophisticated weaponry, intelligence, good communications, and sound tactics and strategy. Both countries are built on a
hierarchy of ethnic groups which are themselves settlers. The struggle
for survival and legitimacy are endemic to both and they hold on to
occupied territories (South Africa - Namibia; Israel – Golan; Gaza
and West Bank). Their relations to the UN are similar and they are
deeply suspicious of the rest of the international community. Their
'siege mentality' and decision to survive through internal military self-
sufficiency coupled with their religious zeal and boldness in action on
third world 'terrorism', are common patterns in both countries.

John Keegan, a leading British defence analyst, believes that the Afrikaners can hold on for years.[11] In March 1987, Israel received considerable attention in the United States and World press on their military connection with South Africa. On 31 March, Piet Marais, as Head of Armscor, said, in response to Israel's indication that it would not sign a new defence contract with Pretoria, 'My country is not dependent on Israel.'[12] This may very well have a ring of truth, considering the numerous indicators that show Armscor's increased propensity for developing fairly sophisticated systems in-house. Nevertheless, whether Marais had become emboldened because of Armscor's capabilities or he was speaking in order to lead the audience into believing in a diminished Israeli role, one cannot be certain. However, in the light of the past Israeli-South African connection, it is most likely that their relationship will continue in a less overt manner. In line with the theme of the 'prevailing mood' in Pretoria, significant boasting of the 'success in defeating the arms embargo' and 'its weapons industry was so advanced it was now the third largest foreign-currency earner after mining and agriculture', has become prevalent.[13] Viewing themselves as a mirror image of Israel, South Africa has, by design, made an all-out effort to become self-sufficient. This independence, in Pretoria's view, can only come through the

PLATE 4.7   XTPI Helicopter

PLATE 4.8   Amil 20 Kwevoel Vehicle

PLATE 4.9   Tenkvervoerder

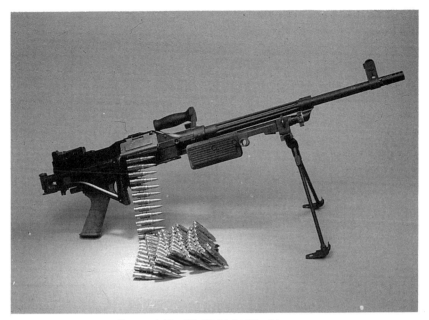

PLATE 4.10   SS-77 Light Machine-gun

acquisition of sophisticated and technologically superior weapons systems. The British Broadcasting Corporation (BBC) stressed this weapons independence on 2 April 1987.[14] 'The list (armaments production list) testifies to foresight, thorough planning and innovative development. It is ironic that it was the weapons boycott that led to it and to South Africa becoming a foremost manufacturer and exporter of arms...'[15] Armscor's policy of planned evolution is following the pattern that had its genesis in the 1960s. First, in the early '60s, as we have already seen, Pretoria was dependent solely on outside sources for armaments. The pressure of the boycott led to Armscor moving to the second phase, whereby the concentration was on negotiations to obtain external manufacturing licences with the intent to manufacture arms locally. It is now in the third phase, which concentrates on two elements – the design and manufacture of its own unique weapons systems and the upgrading and re-fitting of existing systems. General Denis Earp, Chief of the South African Air Force, in an ebullient and confident mood when speaking at the unveiling of the Cheetah said:

> We cannot allow ourselves to be dependent on a possibly hostile supplier ... if we cannot get assistance, we can go it alone. If we have to, we can do it ... we have done it in the past and here, once again, is the proof in front of us. Every time we do a little more, we learn a

little more ... the Atlas Aircraft Corporation has not reached the stage where its only restrictions are time and money.[16]

A Success Story?

If one believes that this is a success story of an underdog who utilises ingenious manipulation within the international community and considerable effort internally, then one is apt to give substantial credibility to Pretoria for acting in its own defence. Moral assertions notwithstanding, it is difficult to defame Armscor's innovative thoroughness. Were the attempts to isolate South Africa misguided? Obviously, this is an emotive and controversial question. The facts show that the isolationist campaign has been a failure in a specifically limited sense, that is, when viewed within the context of the attempt to limit South Africa's military capability. All indicators point to a South African Defence Force that is now stronger, more self-sufficient and better prepared for conventional and counter-insurgency warfare than before the embargoes were imposed. What price has been paid by Pretoria for self-sufficiency in armaments? It hardly seems a burden for the nation. As a matter of fact, it might very well be a plus in the light of the astronomical amount of money now being spent worldwide on armaments. As a supplier, Armscor's balance sheet may be continually in the black if this trend continues. For instance, the Iraq/Iran war has consumed more material than any other conflict since the Vietnam war. The two combatants have acquired over $70 billion worth of weapons and material, including non-lethal supplies, since the war started.[17] According to *Business Week*, Pretoria is earning a share, albeit small in aggregate terms, in this part of the world armaments market:

> South Africa, too, plays a secret but critical role in sustaining Iran's war effort. Armscor, the state arms monopoly, has two major ammunition plants, each producing 300,000 to 400,000 155 mm artillery shells a year. That clearly exceeds the needs of South Africa's own military. 'The South Africans do not need that kind of capacity', said Mark A. Bely, technical director of Mecar, a US owned arms company in Belgium. 'Who does? Iran, that's who.'
>
> Intelligence sources say that Armscor, which manufactures a version of France's Mirage jet fighters to South Africa's military, is also now making spare parts for the U.S. F-4 Phantom jet fighters that the Iranian regime inherited. The South African Government officially declines to comment on arms sales to Iran. But, says the Armscor executive, 'when you are a pariah country, people call you.'[18]

It is estimated that Armscor sells an estimated $300 million worth of artillery ammunition annually to Iran.[19] *Armada International* points out another exceptionally lethal type of bomb being supplied by South Africa:

> ... The South African Armscor CB470 has been used operationally by Iraq in the Gulf War. It weighs 450 kg and contains 40 spherical 6.2 kg bomblets. Like the Alpha bomb developed in Rhodesia in the early 1970s, these bomblets are designed to bounce from any surface, giving an air-burst. They are ejected by cartridge, armed 0.9 sec. later and detonated 0.65 sec. after impact. The CB470 can be released as low as 100 ft (30 m) and provides fragmentation over an area of 17,500 m².[20]

In the light of the sheer quantity of arms being transhipped to Iran and Iraq, how can governments pretend not to support the traffic in arms, at least tacitly, despite the United Nations embargo? It is almost ludicrous to suppose that moral pronouncements override the national interests of states in their pursuit to supply weapons in the Iran–Iraq conflict. Whether governments' interests lie in generating revenue or in ideological self-gratification, the huge armaments imports by the combatants cannot go unnoticed by these governments. For whatever reason, the major suppliers – Britain, China, France, Israel, South Africa, Vietnam, Brazil and the Soviet Union have their hand in the cash box, while the United States winks. Even the so-called neutral countries – Sweden, Switzerland and Austria are caught up as instrumentalists in fuelling the war. Of a higher concern, however, may be the hypocrisy of it all.

5

Statutes of the Republic of South Africa

In order fully to understand the internecine relationships within the South African Defence establishment, the reader *must* as a minimum, be aware of those statutes of the Republic of South Africa that have raised Armscor to political ascendancy, namely; Defence Special Accounts Act, Number 6 of 1974; Armaments Development and Productions Act, Number 57 of 1968 with amendments through to 1982; and Simulated Armaments Transactions Prohibition Act, Number 2 of 1976. These acts are germane to an understanding of the nexus of legality, statutory power, exclusionary rights, financial flexibility and abolition of bureaucratic procedures as they pertain to Armscor. All too little has been written about them.

Defence Special Account Act

The Defence Special Account Act (DSAA) established an account known as the Special Defence Account (SDA). These monies are to be appropriated by Parliament for the requirements of the South African Defence Force 'if the Minister of Defence in consultation with the Minister of Finance deems it necessary in the public interest...'. Unlike United States budgetary accounts, the SDA is allowed by statute to accrue funds *ad infinitum*.

The Chief of the South African Defence Force acts as 'Accounting Officer' in administering the monies in the account. That responsibility is established in section 2(b) of the SDAA:

85

(b) The chief executive officer of the Armaments Corporation of South Africa, Limited, established by section 2 of the Armaments Development and Production Act, 1968 (Act No. 57 of 1968) hereinafter referred to as the Corporation, shall be charged with the responsibility of administering and accounting for monies paid from the account by the Corporation in connection with its special defence activities and purchases referred to in subsection (2) (a) of this section.[1]

The monies in the account are to be utilised to defray 'such special defence activities and purchases of the South African Defence Force and the Corporation as the Minister of Defence may from time to time approve'. The interpretation of 'such' has led to much acrimonious debate in Parliament. In addition, the account is to be audited by the Auditor General. However, the difficulty arises not in the amount for military expenditure but in the credible audit trail that guarantees that a specific amount is, in fact, spent on a specific military expenditure.

Critics have inferred that monies are in practice diverted for other than stated expenditures both within the Defence Force and Armscor. These expenditures then become 'secret' and circumvent the intention of Parliament in establishing the DSAA. In addition, the Minister of Finance (according to the Act) plays a minimal role of approving the spending of the monies inferred in the DSAA, and has minimal say as to the worthiness of the expenditure. This may very well be splitting hairs, since both the Minister of Finance and Defence are part of State President Botha's cabinet. Frankel, although not examining the statute itself, draws a firm conclusion on this 'unofficial defence budget':

> ... perhaps most importantly, the politically indicative quality of the defence budget is skewed by the fact that a considerable proportion of South Africa's defence expenditure is actually laundered through a secret Defence Special Account, under the direct authority of the prime minister* and beyond the realms of state audit. Originally established in 1952 to facilitate the purchase of arms on the world market, this initially small fund has escalated in size to the point where today in sheer quantitative terms, it enjoys the status of an *unofficial defence budget*†. ...[2]

---

*Prime Minister is now the State President.
†Author's emphasis.

Armaments Development and Production Act
No. 57 of 1968*

The politico-military-economic 'power' nexus of Armscor had its genesis in the Armaments Development and Production Act. The Act gives Armscor wide-reaching and exclusionary powers which, over the years, have led to the establishment of a monolithic body for the procurement, manufacture and exporting of weapon systems. In the light of the share of the Defence Budget it represents and the considerable number of industries which are dependent, to a varying extent, upon arms contracts, Armscor makes a significant impact upon the South African economy.

This twenty-seven page explicit and detailed statute lays down the general powers of the Corporation, vesting rights, specific and extensive powers of the Minister of Defence in relation to export, marketing, import, conveyance, development and manufacture. It gives the Minister rights to information on any aspect of the manufacture, marketing and procurement of armaments and specifically lays out the 'Offences' in connection with the development, manufacture and marketing of armaments by others. In addition, the Minister has *carte blanche* inspection rights. The Act covers the responsibilities of the Board of Directors of Armscor and various functional committees. Far-reaching powers are given to the Minister and to Armscor by the loose phraseology of the Act when specifying the delegation of powers, share capital, loans, limitation of liability of the State, exemption from duties or fees, funds of the Corporation and its finances. Of ominous consequence could be a 'hidden' agenda emanating from that lack of precision in certain sections of the Act. For instance, Section 7B:

7B Funds of Corporation – (1) The funds of the corporation shall consist of –
(a) the share capital mentioned in section 6;
(b) monies appropriated by Parliament in order to enable the corporation to perform its functions;
(c) monies raised, borrowed or obtained by the corporation in terms of section 6Λ(1);
(d) monies obtained from any other source.
(2) The corporation may receive donations or contributions from any person and shall use any monies so acquired for such purposes and

---

*This Act was amended by Armaments Development and Production Amendments Acts, No. 65 of 1972, No. 20 of 1977, No. 5 of 1978, No. 86 of 1980, No. 56 of 1982 and Finance Act, No. 21 of 1980.

in accordance with such conditions as the donors or contributors may specify.

(3) The corporation may utilise any balance of its monies remaining at the end of any financial year of the corporation for any expenses in connection with the performance of its functions.

(S.7B inserted by s.7 of Act 20 of 1977)[3]

This open-ended section gives Armscor over-reaching financial flexibility. The question arises whether this type of flexibility becomes open to challenge in terms of it becoming a self-serving instrument for individuals in prominent positions or a streamlined, unaccountable *modus operandi* for corporate executives to enhance the managerial efficiency of Armscor by eliminating the ever-present, tortuously slow-moving bureaucracy of the South African Government. Furthermore it makes it possible to circumvent certain Parliamentary functionaries who, as watchdogs of the budget, come into conflict with the Defence establishment.

It seems ironic that whereas loose phraseology in some sections of the Act, as discussed above, should provide that element of flexibility which can develop into power, the five pages which cover the rules and regulations relating to employment are very precise and it is from that very precision that the Corporation derives its power in that field.

There are definitive explanatory sections on employees' associations, constitution of employees' associations, disputes between employees and employers, Settlement Board, document submission and the finality of the decision of the Settlement Board. However, despite all of this procedural legal jargon in the statute, the real substance is promulgated in section 8G:

8G. Prohibition of strikes – (1) No employee or other person shall instigate a strike or incite any employee to take part in or continue a strike, and no employee shall take part in a strike or in the continuation of a strike.

(2)(a) When an employee employed in a particular department, branch or division of the corporation or a subsidiary company is charged with having taken part in a strike or in the continuation of a strike in contravention of the provisions of subsection (1) and it is proved that concerted action as defined in paragraph (b) took place in that department, branch or division during the period covered by the charge and that the accused was at any time during that period engaged upon work or a type of work with respect to the performance of which such a departure from standards, methods, procedures or practices as referred to in subparagraph (i) of that paragraph had occurred:

(i) such concerted action shall be deemed to constitute a retardation of the progress of work or an obstruction of work as contemplated in the definition of 'strike' in section 1;

(ii) The accused shall be deemed to have taken part in such concerted action unless he proves that he was opposed to that action and in fact took no part in it and that during the period covered by the charge he openly dissociated himself from that action.[4]

The statute goes on to state that those who contravene certain provisions in the Act, 'shall be guilty of an offence and liable on conviction to a fine ...' The act is so written as to assume a permanent war footing for the Republic.

The State President has the power to 'make regulations in regard to – location of the corporation ..., the manner of calculating the price at which and the circumstances in which armament shall be supplied ..., generally, all matters for which he deems it necessary or expedient to make regulations in order to achieve the objects of this Act.' In addition, the State President can regulate secrecy, voting procedures and quorum, keeping books of account and *the contents of auditors' or other reports to be furnished to the Minister by the board.** One can see the all-encompassing and sweeping powers that the State President can wield and, in fact, rightfully does so in the execution of his office.

There is a specific section that prohibits the disclosure of certain information:

> 11A. Prohibition of disclosure of certain information: (1) No person shall disclose to any person any information in relation to the acquisition, supply, marketing, importation, export, development, manufacture, maintenance or repair of or research in connection with armaments by, for, on behalf of or for the benefit of the corporation or a subsidiary company, except on the written authority of the Minister or of a person authorised thereto by the Minister. ...[5]

Anyone found guilty of violation of this section is subject to heavy fines and imprisonment.

Under this statute, Armscor is *not* subject to the provisions of the Companics Act, 1926, 'or any other law relating to companies, shall not apply with reference to the corporation'. In sum, Armscor is exempt from provisions of certain laws and as such, has a unique position within the politico-military-economic structure of the Republic of South Africa.

---

*Author's emphasis.

It is interesting to note that many informed sources complain about defence expenditures, the Defence Special Account, the uncontrollability of Armscor, the 'legislative veil of secrecy' surrounding it and the powers of the State President, Minister of Defence and Chairman of Armscor, yet these same sources never seem to focus on the reason for that power – the law as written in the statutes. 'Total onslaught' and 'total strategy' notwithstanding, the aforementioned Acts have given ominous power to selected individuals and groups. Lord Acton's dictum is germane in that, 'Power corrupts and absolute power corrupts absolutely.' Nevertheless, except for some minor brouhahas, the absolute powers inherent in the statutes have been overwhelmingly directed toward the quickest means to get to the end, i.e. an unencumbered armaments and weapons manufacturing body that incorporates those technical, research and development skills that will satisfy South Africa's needs for internal armament and generate export revenues through sales of arms and weapons systems. If one looks at Armscor's mandate, one must agree that the corporation is fulfilling this mandate. To what degree Armscor will remain in profit in the immediate future is a source of conjecture. The absolute expenditure on weapons systems is difficult, at best, to determine because of the 'covering shield' provided by the phraseology of the statutes. However, we are not concerned in this book with the application of any moral yardstick to the actions of the South African Government but with the examination of empirical data relating to Armscor and, quite simply, to show why and how the Corporation 'ticks'.

The present statutes seem to fit like a glove on the personalities of the power brokers in Armscor, the State President P.W. Botha, the Minister of Defence, Magnus Malan and the Head of Armscor, Commandant Piet Marais. All are dedicated nationalists, vehemently anti-communist, willing to incorporate the *laager* against the 'forces of evil', possess strong personal loyalties to one another and have an overriding and compelling drive to stem the 'total onslaught'. The incessant will and dedication of this triumvirate in the defence of the Republic, as they see it, seems to over-shadow deeply any concern there might be for personal financial gain through power vested in them by statute. As at the time of writing, scandals in this regard have been exceedingly rare, despite the scope and independence of Armscor. Indeed, despite any misgivings voiced about the Armscor triumvirate in the Western and selected internal South African press, the fact remains that the three perceive themselves as true patriots in a cause that will one day vindicate all the acrimonious rhetoric directed against the South African system. The zeal and determination of this group (and others involved in the work of Armscor in the past) have given Armscor the personal impetus needed to overcome seemingly inordinate odds in becoming almost self-sufficient in arms production and procurement.

A perusal of the Armaments and Production Act, incorporated as Appendix C on page 143, will not only give the reader a clearer understanding of the Act but will enable him or her to appreciate fully the inherent powers bestowed on selected individuals and bodies by statute*. Additionally, a study of the Act and the amendments to it clearly shows an evolutionary increase in power for the leading actors. This, coupled with the political mentality of the ruling Nationalist Party, as portrayed in the nuances of the Act, should give one a clearer perspective of the organisational prowess of Armscor, of the political elite and of the deep-seated beliefs of the power brokers. This particular statute is but a small, albeit important link in understanding the inherent power of a single corporate body – Armscor.

Simulated Armaments Transactions Prohibition Act No. 2 of 1976

This little known Act prohibits unauthorised persons from purporting to represent the State or Armscor in armaments transactions. More importantly, the Act, in essence, prohibits anyone from dealing in arms except through Armscor – a rather simple and unique way of further entrenching the power of the Corporation. Section 2 gives a litany of items that is punishable by fine and/or prison or both:

> 2. Prohibition of simulated acts in relation to armaments. – Any person who, in the Republic or elsewhere, in any manner whatsoever purports to acquire from any person, whether as the agent or authorised representative of or otherwise on behalf of the State, the board of the corporation, armaments, any information in regard thereto or patents, licences, concessions, rights of manufacture or the like in relation to armaments, or so to inquire about the availability of armaments, any information in regard thereto or patents, licences, concessions, rights of manufacture or the like in relation to armaments, or so to negotiate for the establishment of agencies in the Republic with regard to armaments, patents, licences, concessions, rights of manufacture or the like in relation to armaments shall be guilty of an offence ...[6]

---

*See Appendix C.

It is interesting to note that all laws, by law, must be written in English and Afrikaans and normally are gazetted in the different languages on alternate pages. The following notation is usually affixed to the English translation: (Afrikaans Text signed by the State President). It should also be noted that when statutes become operable it is most difficult to rescind them due to a built-in constituency, often a minority, that plays havoc within Parliament. In South Africa it is easier to make laws than to nullify them. With this logic in mind, armament statutes should become most difficult to amend downward or to rescind.

6

Armscor's Information Link

Armscor's unique library, located on the corner of Visagie and Paul Kruger Avenues in Pretoria, presents one, upon examination, with a clear part of the mosaic that surrounds the growing prominence of the Armaments Corporation of South Africa Ltd. Situated on the 16th floor of the Lisbon Bank Building, under exceptional tight security where a previously cleared bona fide visitor must sign-in, be identified, questioned and then wait for an escort to arrive. You are issued a KRYGKOR (ARMSCOR) numbered BESOEKER (VISITOR) badge which must be affixed to your person. Once accepted as a bona fide visitor, you are treated exceptionally well. The problem is receiving the clearance to the status of bona fide visitor. When your escort arrives and identifies you, you enter the building through two-glass electronically controlled doors. The library itself is a hub of efficiency, staffed by over twenty people. If you are fortunate enough to be granted access to it, you are under constant supervision, not so much because as an outsider you are an anomaly, but due to the physical layout. There are six hundred and fifty up-to-date periodicals, the overwhelming majority of which are geared towards those who are technologically weapons oriented, such as Armscor engineers and executives.* Hydraulics, pneumatics, solid state circuits, oceanic engineering, electromagnetic compatability, microwave theory and cybernetics are but a few of the subjects covered. Of course, there are also the normal political, economic and

---

*Krygkorbiblioteek Tydskriflys as of 2 June 1988.

93

current events journals that one would find in other libraries. A vast quantity of material is systematically catalogued to provide an almost mind-boggling array of data on worldwide systems pertaining to armaments, defence, military proving grounds and logistical/maintenance/testing commands.

In addition, material is available on armament technology and the latest engineering break-throughs pertaining to weapons and computer-generated armaments test results. Some of the latest information on American weapons testing is available as well as reports on voluminous material from the United States Air Force Systems Command such as contract data management. Reams of United States Defence Supply Agency information as well as United States Navy Technical data are available. One can find, for instance, information on any type of pyrotechnic to include complete drawings, functional charts and engineering blueprints. It becomes readily obvious to the layman that pyrotechnical items could easily be manufactured with the proper plant and tooling facilities.

Projecting The Image

As one of many functions of the library, the staff continually collates all information as it pertains to Armscor from the odd six hundred and fifty periodicals previously mentioned. This material is chronologically placed in working binders. This in itself is not of particular importance but the 'tracking' of that information becomes of critical importance to the public relations department of Armscor. Their goal is to ensure that an image of competence and reliability is projected to a worldwide arms community through international and national media sources. Armscor claims sales to 26 countries and is pushing hard to increase this number.[1] News articles on its weapons systems, in addition to heavy advertisements in various defence journals, attest to the emphasis placed by the Corporation on Public Relations. The July/August 1987 National Defense magazine article entitled 'South African Composite Armor', is a factual account, nevertheless, the hand of Armscor's Public Relations Department is evident:

> Composite armor for fighting vehicles, able to resist 'all but the most advanced shells' is now being produced in South Africa... South Africa is now able to supply its needs of small arms and has moved up into the manufacture of heavy calibre weapons as well.

The establishment of the South African weapons industry was a result of the current international arms boycott ... and has made the nation the world's fifth biggest exporter of defense equipment. Products now available include tanks, armored cars, mine-proof vehicles, missile-armed patrol boats, and aircraft.[2]

From the tenth largest exporter in early 1987 to 'the world's fifth biggest exporter...' by mid-1987 smacks of an excellent blend of Public Relations and Armscor panache. Press conferences are periodically held to extol the virtues of Armscor. The announcement of the PUMA programme is a case in point:

In the future, South Africa will be able to manufacture PUMA helicopters without having to import any parts. At a recent press conference, the South African firm Atlas Aircraft Corporation displayed a PUMA 330 on which most of the moving parts and the airframe had been manufactured in South Africa. Some of the parts and components that can now be manufactured in South Africa were also shown individually. The helicopter on display, the XTP-1 (Experimental Test Platform 1) is one of at least two that are being used for the testing, qualification, and integration of South African parts, components, and systems.[3]

However, much of Armscor's Public Relations material contains a great deal of truth – like, 'The PUMA XTP-1 is armed with a computer-controlled machine gun ... even more important than the local manufacture of such parts is the local manufacture of the machines used to fabricate such parts....'[4] Armscor's advertisements are colourful, hard-hitting, stress combat realiability and appeal to the eye. Kentron's large headlines, 'We don't only make missiles', in the August 1987 *Kentron News* will eventually be part of a worldwide campaign to attract high level technical personnel. Most Armscor advertisements are quick to catch the eye. There is no doubt that competition is keen in the international arms market. A perusal of the many high gloss periodicals on the market are prima-facie indicators of worldwide annual multi-billion dollar arms sales. Armscor has learned quickly. Their advertisement campaign centres on a five-pronged theme, thus:

EYE CATCHING PHOTO	CAPTION	PICTURE OF ARMAMENT(S) FOR SALE
PORCUPINE	'OPEN FOR ACTION'	– CLUSTER BOMB, CB470
RHINOCEROS	'MOBILITY IS HALF THE BATTLE'	– SELF-PROPELLED 155 MM HOWITZER, G6
LION	'UNIQUENESS IS OUR STRENGTH LIKE THE LION OF TIMBAVATI – ARMSCOR, ONE OF A KIND'	– G6 HOWITZER – GA1 MACHINE GUN – CB470 CLUSTER BOMB
COBRA	'STRIKEABILITY'	– AUTOMATIC GUN, 20 MM, GA1
FIGHTER PLANE	'WHY WE NEED PEOPLE WHO HAVE THEIR SIGHTS SET ON TOMORROW'	– INTRA-COCKPIT AIRCRAFT SIGHT (PERSONNEL ADVERTISEMENT)

These same advertisements are printed in Arabic and Spanish when the target audience warrants it. Armscor's eye for expanding is not only found in its stepped-up advertisement campaign but in its vast building construction expansion phase, particularly in and around Pretoria.

A Microcosm of the United States Library of Congress

The Armscor library serves the staff of Armscor well. It plays a small but vital role not only in maintaining South Africa's armaments industry in its present position but in providing a link towards projecting it into the front rank of international arms exporters. One could say, 'a library is a library, is a library', however, the significance of this one lies not so much in the library *per se*, but in the overall attention to detail that the management of Armscor's demands of itself and its staff. This is just one of many facets of the Armscor organisation that aids it in maintaining an edge in a very competitive business where today's state-of-the-art easily becomes tomorrow's horse-drawn carriage.

The functional process at the library not only provides the selected few with information on weapons systems but represents a particular effort to get selected documentation from worldwide sources. For instance, R.A. Nellor's *How to get it – a guide to defence-related documents*, although printed in 1973, needs minimal updating. The content covers technical documents and related material that scientists and engineers ordinarily have to use.

One might compare the Armscor library staff to a microcosm of the staff of the U.S. Library of Congress – the difference being that the Armscor staff conducts its work in a specialised environment, instead of a general environment. In doing so, they provide numerous services but little in-depth analysis. An individual from any of the Armscor subsidiaries can request either a specific piece of literature or all available information on a specific subject matter. The staff collates this material and forwards a copy to the requesting individual whether he or she be at SWARTKLIP in the Cape Flats or at INFOPLAN or ELOPTRO in Pretoria or Kempton Park. An on the spot survey showed an impressive list of some 25 packages of copied material, covering a wide range of technological interest and disciplines, all prepared for despatch on a single day to Armscor employees throughout the Corporation.

A computer information system connects all participating defence information systems to the Armscor library. This enables it to have ready access not only to a defence related information bank but to other technical information as well. For instance, the 195 page book *Suid-Afrikaanse Krygsmag* by H. Heitman, 1985, could readily be accessed through the computer system if not found in the card catalogue. This speedy reference system would show that it was held at Kentron Industries.

The 'Show and Tell' Programme

An extensive catalogued coloured photograph and coloured slide file is available on all internal weapons systems and selected component parts of these systems. The twenty-thousand coloured prints are systematically categorised by type of weapons system, chronologically numbered by year and coded by sequence of photo taken in a specific year. For instance, if one comes across a photo labelled *SAMIL 20 BULLDOG (CN83-1489)*, it is possible to discern what the subject matter looks like, what year the photo was taken (1983) and what number of photo it was in that year (1,489). In this way, on quick notice, the photo laboratory can speedily reproduce a coloured slide or a photo of the SAMIL 20 BULLDOG. This becomes important not only in the internal workings of Armscor but it is particularly important in the export of weapons systems. A client may want to see a pictorial running guide of all the modifications made to a weapons system since its inception. Or, he or she may want a pictorial comparison of different systems. The flexibility of this photo and coloured slide file gives Armscor the wherewithall to produce almost instantaneously, any array of photos/slides for an arms buyer. Of particular note, in this comprehensive catalogue, is the graphic display through coloured slides and photos of the internal mechanisms and sub-systems of selected armaments. One staff member is responsible for the continual updating and cataloguing of this 'show and tell' programme which has paramount importance for the public relations and marketing departments in their ceaseless efforts to increase Armscor's share of the international armaments market.

This unique library is programmed to move into Armscor's new head office complex outside Pretoria. The place of its new location is designed to facilitate an even more productive and responsive information link.[5]

7

The Future of Armscor – An Assessment

If the assumption is made that South Africa will not abandon its current form of government to any great degree, it follows that the South African Defence Force will have to maintain its technological edge over its adversaries in the future. Although only a regional power, South Africa demonstrated its capability to present a respected conventional force against the Soviet/Cuban-led offensive into Southern Angola in October/November 1987. Not only did the Defence Force perform well and aid UNITA in defeating the 14 brigade FAPLA force, but it also showed its military prowess in the art of mobile warfare through the effective use of its up-to-date communications system. In addition, 'Pretoria's Praetorians', with their sophisticated G6, 155 mm Gun-Howitzers were exceptionally apt at the use of artillery. These guns took a crippling toll of the Angolan forces and caused Soviet loss of face. Many academics predicated in the media that a South African all-out-war with the Soviets was a strong possibility because the Defence Force had been 'kicking the shins of a giant', Professor Frost believes that 'there is no way the Soviets are going to give up or retreat in the face of a small power like South Africa when, in 1975, they won the first round against a superpower like the United States'.*

A number of South African academics, knowledgeable in Southern African regional politico-military affairs, have expressed deep concern over the muscle flexing of the Defence Force against the Soviet-led FAPLA forces. Such notables as Dr. Sarah Pienaar, an authority on

*Professor Mervyn Frost, Head of the University of Natal's Department of International Relations, as quoted in the *Sunday Tribune*, 15 Nov. 87.

Soviet affairs from UNISA; Professor Frost, Professor John Barratt of the South African Institute of International Affairs; Professor Peter Vale, Director of Rhodes University Institute for Social and Economic Research; have all expressed deep concern about the implications of the SADF involvement in Angola.[1] Less sanguine was Professor Mike Hough, Director of the Institute for Strategic Studies, University of Pretoria. 'Ultimately, of course, it is political and strategic interests that determine the issue of South African involvement, and not so much morality.' He goes on, '... South Africa can certainly not remain aloof from regional developments ... there is some parallel between U.S. involvement in Grenada, and South Africa's involvement in Angola.'[2] However, it is ironic that many international analysts believe the chances for negotiated settlement in Angola are improving. Unfortunately for South Africa, the conventional wisdom is that Pretoria will be frozen out of the deal.

Statements by Pretoria are strongly worded against the alleged communist onslaught in Southern Africa. Despite being warned of 'being sucked into a conventional war with the Soviet Union', Magnus Malan, the Minister of Defence, said that the South African Defence Force was committed to throwing its full weight into the war.[3] Cuban leader Fidel Castro has gone on record to the effect that he is considering stepping up military support for Angola's embattled communist regime. This rhetoric may be hollow in the light of the Soviets' assessment of possible negotiations, allowing them to bow out gracefully without their tails between their legs. On a more realistic note, Cuban troops are funded externally at no cost to Castro and intelligence reports indicate their dissatisfaction and low morale. Furthermore, the cost to Cuba of bringing home upwards of 40,000 troops would add to Castro's already deepening economic woes. They would have to be employed and absorbed into an already weak economic fabric of society.

Despite the claims and counter-claims of all regional and international bodies with an interest in Southern Africa, and despite their public declaration with regard to their conditions to meet the spirit of United Nations Resolution 435, South Africa's near term interests are not served by a Cuban withdrawal from Angola. To suggest this may very well fly in the face of conventional wisdom, yet unofficial sources point to other considerations. First, Cuban forces changed their operational military tactics since the latter part of 1987 when the Soviets decided on the ill-fated thrust towards Jonas Savimbi's UNITA headquarters at Jamba that was blunted at Mavinga and finally degenerated into a standoff at Cuito Cuanavale. At this time Cuban forces were used in static positions freeing FAPLA forces for offensive operations. These Angolan forces proved to be less than professional in combat environments – a plus for the South African Defence Force.

Since the June 1988 débâcle at Mavinga, Cuban troops moved to within 12 kilometres of the strategically located Ruacana hydro-electric scheme at Calueque, Angola which provides Owamboland in Namibia with electricity and water. These troops were reinforced by 10,000 Cubans who landed previously at the Southern Angolan port of Namibe. Almost unimpeded by South African forces, the Cubans simultaneously lengthened the runways at Xangongo airfield and deployed sophisticated weaponry at another airfield at Cahama. The joint FAPLA, the South West African People's Organisation (SWAPO), and Cuban move south established bases at Cahama, Xangongo and Caiundo. The Cubans have taken over the Angolan army's role of providing a protective shield and support for SWAPO guerrillas. Cuba's role as a possible 'spoiler' in the 1988 peace negotiations between Angola, South Africa, and Cuba, under United States mediation and Soviet direct interest, is a plus for Pretoria. Secondly, the Cubans are generally disgruntled and the cost is becoming burdensome for both the Soviets and the Angolans. Thirdly, a *quid pro quo* of 'free elections' in Namibia for Cuban withdrawal is not in the interest of Pretoria, particularly if UNTAG plays a dominant role in overseeing them. If a less than friendly government takes power in Namibia, in Pretoria's view the goestrategic position of South Africa becomes untenable. There is no longer a buffer zone, the entrenchment of SWAPO in Namibia becomes a self-fulfilling prophecy, the cut-off of ready access by the South African Defence Force through the Caprivi Strip to countries who harbour ANC cadres and the possibility of a strong Soviet presence in Namibia become realities in South African eyes. Fourthly, a Cuban withdrawal would place undue international focus on South Africa and its manoeuvrings on the acceptance or non-acceptance of the conditions of Resolution 435. This would put South Africa in a 'no win' situation, viewed from the perspective that a state's actions are based on its national interests. It is quite simply not in Pretoria's national interests to have an 'unacceptable government' in Windhoek. The South Africans would not be inclined to accept much less than the present existing National Assembly type government in South West Africa. In that government, the legislative power is vested in sixty-two members from six political parties – Democratic Turnhalle Alliance

(DTA), Labour Party, National Party (NP), Liberation Front, South West Africa National Union (SWANU), and Swapo Democrats (SWAPO-D). The executive power is vested in a cabinet of eight ministers assisted by eight deputy ministers. The chairmanship of the cabinet rotates every three months in alphabetical order. The Central Government consists of sixteen departments.

If one assesses the Southern African situation and numerous public and private statements by Pretoria's cabinet ministers, coupled with open source factual defence spending and numerous discernable national and international trends, it is easy to project (not predict) a near future scenario for South Africa which includes a large role for Armscor.*

The situation is perceived as such by the Nationalist Party of South Africa that total political franchise for the black population would mean an end to the 'white tribe'. As a matter of concern for Pretoria is the negative support coming from certain circles for South Africa's twin policies of de-regulation and privatisation. Although the business community favours these policies, the most powerful Trade Union Federation in the country, COSATU, strongly opposes it. COSATU believes that the policies are 'a political attack on the living standards of all workers'. The ANC's Freedom Charter flies in the face of privatisation and de-regulation. The Charter leads strongly toward nationalisation in the form of 'Ownership of the people as a whole'.[4] This includes mineral wealth, banks, monopoly industry and trade. Quite frankly, this creates the most profound alarm in Pretoria. In fact, the Manifesto of the Azanian People goes even further, stating that *all* will be owned and controlled by the Azanian peoples (this can be taken literally to mean the exclusion of whites). Although black opinion makers will be heard and tolerated in the near future, there is absolutely no indication that white power and decision making will be eroded, despite the apparent growth of unified black organisations such as COSATU and UDF. Money, education, means of enforcement, intelligence networks, strong vertical and horizontal organisational structures and a non-quantifiable zeal of the Afrikaner are the *prima facie status quo* power indicators. The blacks, on the other hand, are a numbered majority, have strong international

---

*The author wrote numerous similar assessments through the medium of politico-military simulations while head of the Politico-Military Division, Studies, Analysis and Gaming Agency of the United States Joint Chiefs of Staff, in the Pentagon. These simulations, set in a future time-frame, were not meant to be predictive. However, subsequent events attested to a high percentage of validity.

support and have little to lose, as that number includes only a miniscule lower middle class, at best. However, the black/white issue becomes muddled when other factors are added to the equation: ethnic diversification and its inherent biases, including an existing and sophisticated hierarchy; the inherent lack of a strong and sophisticated insurgency movement within the country; a non-existent monolithic body to speak for non-whites; the apathetic outlook of substantial numbers of blacks (for whatever reason), which saps an all-encompassing revolutionary zeal; and no clear determinants to the type of struggle – class or race, or both. This portends a 'no change' situation in the near future. The only catalyst for change would be a substantial erosion of the *status quo* through an all-encompassing and enforceable economic stranglehold in conjunction with a military blockade. Conventional wisdom does not point in that direction.

Budget

Things are looking up for Armscor, if the 1987/8 South African Defence Budget is anything to go by. The budget has increased by almost 30 per cent, ensuring Armscor a continued domestic 'shot in the arm' through additional arms purchases by the SADF. Further- more, the October/November 1987 Angolan offensive countered by UNITA and the SADF has required an additional need for artillery shells and bombs to replace those that were expended, in addition to some weapons systems losses. These additional budgetary funds have been earmarked chiefly for modernisation, replacement and new research and development procurement programmes.[5] The greater part of the additional funding will go to the Air Force which will no doubt provide substantial contracts to Atlas Aircraft Corporation (Kempton Park), one of Armscor's subsidiaries. Helmoed-Römer Heitman, one of the few well-informed and connected SADF analysts sums up some of the specific immediate future expenditures:

> ... The SAAF will also be spending some of its funds on additional weapon systems for the Cheetah and the other fighters. With a small short-life turbine having been developed in South Africa, it may also be that some of the SAAF funding is going towards the development of stand-off weapons, as predicted some time ago by Armscor's Chairman, Commandant Marais...

> Research and development work for the Army must also still be continuing to close some definite gaps in its armoury. Two of these are a mobile air-defence system and a heavy anti-tank missile. The

large fleet of Eland armoured cars is now also due for replacement, with some of the individual vehicles probably overdue for retirement. A successor to the Olifant main battle tank must also be receiving attention ...[6]

There are strong indications that substantial increases will be incorporated in the 1988/89 budget for the Navy. The modernisation and return to service of the two remaining President Class frigates would give South Africa a useable blue-water force. Of course, a submarine building programme cannot be discounted. As an aside, intelligence sources indicate that the French Indian Ocean fleet, based in Djibouti will have the protection of the Cape route as its major strategic task for the next five years beginning in 1988. This was confirmed by Rear Admiral Michel Lanxande, Commander of France's Indian Ocean fleet in January 1988. The fleet comprises 27 warships and auxiliary vessels, including the aircraft carrier Clemenceau, destroyers, mine-sweepers and most likely at least one nuclear submarine.[7]

The 'Lavi' Connection

Despite disclaimers by Pretoria and Tel Aviv, the South African/Israeli connection still thrives. In particular, more than fifty aeronautical engineers, laid off from the Israeli LAVI fighter aircraft project, arrived in South Africa before December 1987. The strong presumption is that they will be employed by Armscor. Informed sources indicate that Atlas Aircraft Corporation will open a plant near Pretoria to manufacture a scaled-down version of the LAVI.* This version will be in addition to the Cheetah. For obvious reasons, Armscor representatives have denied this as well as denying the employment of Israeli aeronautical engineers. The scaled-down version of the LAVI will most likely use a different engine than the American model previously planned for the LAVI fighter project.

New Weapons and Sites

Armscor's future viability is predicated on sales within the international market. At the 1988 FIDA Arms exhibition in Chile, South Africa unveiled its own 'Sidewinder' missile and a remote-controlled reconnaissance aircraft.

---

*These are Defence Force sources, the names of which the author is not at liberty to divulge.

This new V3C missile is alleged to be on a par with the AIM-9L Sidewinder and the French-built MATRA MAGIC-2. Armscor will boast that twenty-three new technologies are incorporated in the design which is similar in appearance to the MAGIC-2, thereby helping customers who prefer not to be associated openly with South Africa.

The Israeli connection can be surmised in the remotely piloted vehicle (RPV), which has a similar twin-boom tail and pusher propeller to the Israel Aircraft Industries' SCOUT. The RPV's endurance is quoted as 4.5 hours at 100 kilometres range.[8]

Armscor has developed a new artillery testing range in the Copperton area of the North-Western Cape. This is in addition to several owned test sites like Overberg near Bredasdorp, St. Lucia in Northern Natal, the Alkantpan Ballistic Test Site in the Northern Cape and the Eugene Marais site to the West of Pretoria for vehicle testing. The exact cost of Copperton is not available but estimates run into many millions of dollars. The isolated site can easily accommodate missile and long range artillery testing.

A further indication of Armscor's planning for growth in the future is unconfirmed, but reliable information shows that Armscor is producing its own 'Stingers'. The American-made Stinger is an anti-aircraft hand-held missile that has proved its exceptional lethality in Afghanistan and Southern Angola. It is morally certain that UNITA's Jonas Savimbi gave South Africa an American Stinger to be used as a copy for Armscor's prototype.[9]

A People Oriented Organisation

Houwteg (Pty.) Ltd., situated on 500 hectares of land known as Haasvlakte in the Lebanon State Forest, near Houwhoek in the Cape, is Armscor's new think-tank. When completed it will be staffed by advanced-weapons systems scientists and engineers. This will be Armscor's eleventh major subsidiary.* Houwteg (Pty.) Ltd., is envisioned as predominantly a 'brain-oriented' facility and will be closely linked to the missile-testing range at De Hoop on the Bredasdorp coast. Houwteg will perform extensive laboratory simulated test firings for data enhancement before prototype missile launching takes place. Armscor intends, as in the past, to keep development costs as low as

---

*Telcast is a division of Atlas Aircraft. Situated in Kempton Park, it manufactures high-tech castings with special alloys. It is sometimes listed as a separate subsidiary of Armscor but technically it is not.

possible. Its programme of hiring the best minds is intended to do this.

Despite past reports that Armscor has been retrenching some staff, the Corporation is expanding and modernising its facilities. A large new head office is scheduled to be completed by mid-1989 on a site near Pretoria's historic Erasmus Castle. According to the architectural drawings, the ultra-modern, silvery-coloured head office will be situated on twenty-four hectares of landscaped gardens. It will consist of four blocks on different levels, with the highest being eight stories and will be joined by a semi-circular entrance to provide about 50,000 square metres of 'cell' and open-plan offices for about 2,000 employees. Efficiency, image, productivity and security were the overriding reasons for the new structure.

The Lenz explosive factory near Johannesburg will be completely phased out by March of 1989. Lenz, part of the Armscor subsidiary Naschem (Pty.) Ltd., has proved too costly to run. All staff and equipment will be moved to Naschem's Boskop plant near Potchefstroom. Armscor has stated that one of the reasons for the closing was because of a decline in the demand for its products.[10] The real reasons, however, for the move to Boskop were security, safety, consolidation, economy and cost-effective increased productivity.

Armscor's unofficial policy is to promote from within the organisation. The staff of about 23,000 seems highly motivated and competent.*

The Corporation is always looking for innovative ways to keep the staff at a high level of dedication, know-how and ingenuity. Armscor is a leader in the business of upgrading employees' expertise through education and training. 'An average of 65 per cent of all employees of Armscor undergo some form or another of training every year.'[11] The Corporation utilises numerous incentives and rewards to keep the employees content. Obviously, this is not entirely motivated by an altruistic spirit. They are well aware of the need for the staff and employees to be happy in their work if they are to be fully effective and productive.

The Effect of the Soviet Threat

Because of the ever-present threat of the Soviets in the minds of Pretoria's ruling elite there is no need to believe that Armscor's role

---

*Obviously this is a 'hip pocket analysis' on the Author's part, but formal and informal conversations with selected members of Armscor give this impression.

THE FUTURE OF ARMSCOR – AN ASSESSMENT

in South Africa's politico-military structure will decrease. Indeed, all the indications point to an expanded future role for the Armaments Corporation. In the light of the predictions of some international analysts, that South Africa will be 'frozen out' of any deal that may be struck with Angola, Pretoria is keeping a watchful eye on the Soviet's pronouncement that it is anxious for a 'just political solution'.

Andre du Pisani, research director at the South African Institute of International Affairs and an authority on Angola, believes that the 'just' settlement may take the form of a revival of the Alvor agreement of the 70s which could lead to a joint MPLA/UNITA government in Luanda.

According to du Pisani, the Soviets face two alternatives. Either to achieve a political settlement now, although UNITA is in a strong bargaining position after its recent (October/November 1987) military successes against the MPLA, or, alternatively, the Soviets could increase their military involvement, thereby weakening UNITA's position. Either way, according to du Pisani, Savimbi's big problem is legitimacy and he must break the link with Pretoria if he is to become a player in Luanda.[12] Nevertheless, Pretoria's policy is to prepare for any eventuality. This entails keeping its dominant regional power status intact and in fact improving it with more sophisticated and additional armaments. Thus, the role and significance of Armscor will no doubt increase.

The Real Economic Picture

The Southern African Development Co-ordination Conference (SADCC) has failed in its aim to reduce trade links with South Africa. Zimbabwe, Zambia and Mozambique, three of the most vocal demanders for sanctions, have shown little enthusiasm for action in that regard. The scale of the interdependence of countries in Southern Africa has been outlined in a bulletin by the director of the Africa Institute, Mr. Erich Leistner. This makes it fairly clear that it is probably impossible for SADCC to impose sanctions on South Africa because of the inextricable linkages of socio-economic-technical and political bonds. The technological and entrepreneurial skills of South Africa represent an element which effects all transport links. Although the Beira corridor may reduce Zimbabwe's dependence on Pretoria, South Africa's railways and ports handle 90 per cent of Harare's imports and exports. The figures are about 45 per cent for Malawi and Zambia. Only 3 per cent of the South African Transport Services

(SATS) income, which amounts to R300 million annually, comes from these sources. This is a powerful politico-economic weapon in the hands of Pretoria. A total cut-off would not cause even a ripple of damage to South Africa. SATS provides 50 locomotives and 7,800 units of rolling stock to neighbouring countries.

South African Airways maintains and repairs the aircraft of Mozambique, Swaziland, Mauritius, Zimbabwe and Comoros. Over 10 per cent of South Africa's direct exports are to African countries with stronger trade links to Southern African countries except Angola. The importance of this trade for Southern African countries is that it consists mostly of essentials such as fertilisers, veterinary supplies (millions of doses of vaccine for 42 animal diseases are shipped annually), corn and agricultural and mining machinery. Pretoria maintains an indirect hold on Botswana, Lesotho and Swaziland through the South Africa Customs Union which imposes common tariffs on all imports for all four countries. Twenty-five, sixty-five and fifty per cent respectively of their government revenue is provided by South Africa.

What is even more ironic, despite the oil embargo, is that South Africa provides all the petroleum needs of Botswana, Lesotho and Swaziland, 95 per cent to Malawi and 75 per cent to Zaïre. Zimbabwe gets all its aviation fuel and occasional selected imports of petroleum from South Africa. There are approximately 400,000 legally-recognised workers and an estimated one million illegal workers in South Africa from neighbouring countries.

It must be realised that technical supplies and services from South Africa, are not only less expensive but are more suited to the conditions of the continent. South Africa's Gross National Product in comparison to its neighbours is overwhelming. A view on the non-viability of sanctions was stated thus:

> Effective sanctions on South Africa are impossible without the support and co-operation of the neighbouring countries, and at present it would amount to national suicide for any Southern African country to try seriously to impose sanctions of almost any kind.[13]

As a favoured element of the economic scene in South Africa, Armscor will undoubtedly reap the benefits of contributing to a strong and viable economy. South Africa's diverse economic interests are so numerous that the failure of one is easily compensated by increases in others.

Links with the 'Homelands'

Economic links through the 'Homelands' acquisition of weapons systems play a part, although small, in Armscor's overall reach into the armaments market. Some say the Homelands' small military units are an extension of the SADF. Ciskei and Venda have been supplied with West German MBB BO-105 and MBB BK-117 helicopters on arrangement through Armscor, according to un-named but informed sources. Investigation into this matter, as a violation of the United Nations mandatory arms embargo, has been conducted by the World Campaign against Military and Nuclear Collaboration out of Oslo.[14]

Armscor's Accomplishments

If one views the South African armaments industry from its modest beginnings until today, one sees phenomenal growth. There were dark days, of course, until 1966 when P.W. Botha became Minister of Defence. From the acquisition of new subsidiaries to the commissioning in 1981 of one of the world's most advanced nitro-cellulose plants at Krantzkop near Wellington, Armscor has become one of the few weapons manufacturers that utilises mostly local raw materials. As a result, it is also one of the few arms suppliers in the world with a proven track record of self-sufficiency in raw materials.

Armscor has become a major earner of foreign exchange for South Africa. A close symbiotic relationship exists between it and the hundreds of companies involved in armaments production in South Africa. This formidable partnership with the private sector has led to the pooling of the latest technology and research and development efforts. Appendix D provides the reader with many topical highlights of Armscor's accomplishments. These provide a ready and quick non-technical reference to the past performance of the corporation but, nevertheless, these accomplishments are highly indicative of the future capabilities of the Armaments Corporation of South Africa Ltd.

Summary

Armscor's future looks bright, taking into consideration the turmoil in South Africa, the Soviet's interest in the area, Pretoria's stated policy *vis-à-vis* the 'total onslaught', South Africa's past actions based on the perceptions of its national interests, the international climate and the existing internal socio-economic-politico-military framework of South Africa. The only foreseeable future catalyst for change would be the unlikely event of an enforceable economic stranglehold on Pretoria through a military blockade.

The substantial increase in the 1988/89 Defence Budget and the employment of Israeli aeronautical engineers from the defunct Israeli LAVI fighter aircraft project coupled with South Africa's design of new weapons systems and missile-range testing sites as well as Armscor's increased emphasis on people-orientated programmes, all point directly to a growing role for Armscor in the future plans of Pretoria.

The economic picture for South Africa, in reality, looks anything but dim. Trade with Africa will, at worst, remain about the same. One just has to examine trade links with SADCC, and BLS countries and the rest of Africa, as well as international trade with the West. The economic, technical, trade and service links to Southern Africa are inextricably intertwined. The weapons systems produced by Armscor are a proven commodity. Like any existing bureacracy, Armscor will tend to perpetuate itself through growth. The existing posture of the SADF based on Pretoria's foreign policy, the strong likelihood of increased defence spending in the future, Armscor's all-out campaign to increase its share of the international arms market, all point to the future growth and viability of Armscor.

8

Conclusion

Dealing Through Strength

South Africa's annually increasing defence budget and ever increasing taste for highly sophisticated weapons systems, coupled with its national and international political stance backed by numerous official statements and calculated actions, point towards a country that is determined to take a stand through strength. If one examines the statements of Pretoria's pundits closely it is possible to discern a hardening of attitudes between the 1960s and the late 1980s. 'Preparedness programmes' before the 1977 mandatory arms embargo, 'forcing the world to take cognisance', 'total onslaught' and 'total strategy' were not empty phrases intended to impress the international community or South Africans. Pretoria's rhetoric has been transformed into actions. P.W. Botha's theme invariably centres on the 'threat': '... we anticipate the threat and prepare ourselves accordingly. For this reason we have come to expect Armscor and the Defence Force to ensure our security ...'

The debate may continue as to whether the arms embargo 'forced' South Africa into this military position of strength or not. The fact of the matter is that well-documented sources, the existence of sophisticated armaments and the efficient utilisation of these weapons systems in combat, all demonstrate that Pretoria possesses the military means to invoke its regional policy. In this regard, South Africa will deal from strength. Whether this will be sufficient in the light of various actions by the international community and internal upheavals is a matter yet to be decided.

The Consequences of the Arms Embargo

The United Nations arms embargo may very well have been the springboard that vaulted Armscor into prominence. Nevertheless, it must be realised that there has been armament production in South Africa since the Second World War and that small arms, mortars and guns have been manufactured, particularly at the Defence Ordnance Workshop (now Lyttleton Engineering Works). Through various mergers and amalgamations, particularly in light of the United Nations mandatory arms embargo, Armscor emerged to be what it is today. The question must be asked quite pointedly, What did the arms embargo achieve? It certainly has not brought Pretoria to its knees militarily. It was, however, a forum for those who wished to express their distaste for *apartheid.* If success can be measured in terms of reducing South Africa to pariah status, then a success it was. Nevertheless, strident condemnations for over twenty-five years in the United States and internationally have had little effect on Pretoria's arms merchant, Armscor. In retrospect, a very good case can be made to show an opposite effect. First, it forced Pretoria to go underground in its need for weapons procurement and, in some cases, licences. Secrecy was thus necessary, leading eventually to the ultimate, – South Africa's 'legislative veil of secrecy' on all armament matters. Secondly, manipulation became a necessity and quite frankly, the Afrikaner became quite good at it. Trade-offs, third and fourth party invoices, mis-marked freight showing erroneous ports of origin, pay-offs, bribes, mark-ups – anything and everything in order to procure weapons systems during the early part of the embargo. But, obviously these were not one-sided operations. The international market's array of armaments is such that very few clients are excluded, provided they can pay.

The economic marketplace overrides, morality, United Nations resolutions, ideology and diplomatic agreements in most cases. Thirdly, worldwide arms merchants are numerous, competition is stiff, and the production pipeline must be maintained. Not only do countries sell arms on the world market but a large diversified group of arms and weapons manufacturing firms market anything from the new 9 mm pistol recently purchased by the United States Army to the multi-national warplane, Tornado, developed by West Germany, Britain, and Italy. Britain signed defence contracts worth $4 billion in 1985. In 1986, the figure was nearly $9 billion with a first major Saudi contract to buy Tornado planes, and in 1987, contracts totalled an estimated $5.6 billion. Britain out-manoeuvred United States firms who were intent on selling F-18 fighter aircraft to Saudi Arabia. In July 1988, Britain clinched a $17 billion arms deal with the Saudis which included 50 Tornado fighter-bombers. Britain has replaced France as the world's third largest arms supplier. These are but two examples of the many arms contracts that are negotiated annually.

In the case of the 9 mm pistol, Beretta Corporation of Italy was initially awarded the contract based on a vigorous United States Army testing programme. An American firm – Colt, Incorporated – managed to obtain a re-evaluation of the contract through political pressure. United States Army weapons experts overwhelmingly favoured the 9 mm Beretta. The multi-million dollar contract for this sidearm will keep the winning firm in business for years.

As in both examples of the Tornado and the 9 mm pistol, a large contract provides sufficient revenue to open and maintain the production pipeline while additional contracts are being sought. Furthermore, the need for an enormous number of replacement parts recurs over the life-cycle of weapons systems. The manufacturing, number, time of delivery, categorisation, and technical advice involved with these spare parts is known as the logistics tail. Fourthly, the strong trading ties with nations particularly, Great Britain, Germany, the United States and Israel formed strong links in a chain that could not readily be broken. Fifth, South Africa, in its quest for armaments, moved slowly away from procurement into the rehabilitation of existing sub-systems and weapons and, eventually, into the manufacture of its needs. As this process progressed there was less and less need for the procurement of the so-called 'logistics tail' of a weapon system. Armscor, through its subsidiaries, was manufacturing the 'tail' as part of the complete system. Therefore, over a period of time, those countries, particularly in the West, who were not supplying armaments to South Africa, had little leverage when it came to turning off the spigot of the 'logistics tail'. As events have shown, this was a mistake when viewed in the light of controlling South Africa's weapons systems. If a country procures its armaments and is not granted a licence to manufacture replacement parts, it is eventually at the mercy of the seller. In South Africa's case they were given nearly a quarter of a century to build their rather impressive arms industry.

Sixth, the result has been the creation of a very powerful, monolithic arms manufacturer which is indeed, 'a giant in the South African industry'. Its vast network reaches into the engineering and administration of hundreds of small companies during the contractual, prototype and manufacturing phases. Armscor's strong connections with the Pretoria government are manifested in its 'special role' by statutes, the strong personal ties of the triumvirate (Botha, Malan and Marais), its powerful economic position, and its informal role in the State Security System. Seventh, Armscor has now grown into an international arms merchant. In order to prevent the very costly stops and starts inherent in an armaments company, and its subsidiaries, that manufactures for a relative small armed force, it is essential that every effort should be made to maintain the manufacturing pipeline. In order to do this, external buyers are necessary. Thus, Armscor sells to 26 countries and has geared all elements of the Corporation for increased worldwide sales. Some of its weapons systems are touted as state-of-the-art by many international arms and defence experts.

Eighth, not only can Pretoria conduct its regional policy from strength – economic and military, but it has an agency, that by all indications will be an international money maker. In quality and price and as the supplier of complete weapons systems, along with the training it provides, Armscor has a competitive edge in the international arms market.

Finally, Armscor's powers of monopoly, granted by statute, give it almost a life or death hold over the hundreds of small manufacturing firms who produce components and spares for various weapons systems. Although the relationship is a good one, it presents something of a dilemma. The more these firms re-tool to meet the demands of their arms contracts, the worse the consequences of any fall-off in that demand, leading to loss of work. If the export of weapons systems goes into decline, the expensive on-line specialist machinery cannot easily be re-tooled for the production of non-military commodities. On the other hand, if, as seems possible, exports increase and demand remains high, the advantage in economic terms for thousands of workers will be substantial – increasing Armscor's industrial and economic strength.

Political and Economic Factors

To gain a better understanding of Armscor, one must be aware of the political and economic factors within South Africa and also of the social structures inherent in cultures and categorised by law. Very few African countries, if any at all, could have an Armscor moulded in the South African sense. Their infrastructures and economies would not have supported such a venture. A fundamental understanding of the relationships between the military, the economy and the polity is essential in order to grasp the rapid rise to Armscor's 'power position'. Tracing the origins of the arms embargo and its impact, the siege mentality of the Afrikaner (which can represent both a source of strength and degrees of weakness), the military hierarchy and attitude, the world's major gold producer, P.W. Botha (the man, the politician and the pragmatist) and the National Party are all subjects that warrant intense study and cannot be covered adequately in less than thousands of written pages. Nevertheless, all these matters are fundamental to a thorough understanding of the internecine relationship between the Defence Establishment (including Armscor) and Pretoria. This work was designed to take a critical look at Armscor and in doing so this internicine relationship was covered by exposing select occurrences. Collectively, these occurrences indicate strong inter-relationships.

A Military-Industrial Complex

There is a 'military industrial complex' in South Africa albeit a 'lower order version' of the concept as known by the West. (See Grundy's *The New Role of South Africa's Security Establishment*.) However, Grundy says 'Armscor exists solely to improve the material defence capabilities of the State'. While this is true he probably did not realise that Armscor would become an international arms exporter and a substantial revenue generator for Pretoria. The organisation, budget, engineering and technical sophistication, manufacturing entities, interconnective links, contractual arrangements and the production and sale of weapons systems, all in substantial terms, point to a South African 'military industrial complex'. By comparison, not as large and unwieldy as others but, nevertheless, one just the same. This 'complex' could very well prove to be the epitome of efficiency and effectiveness as compared to the American model if Armscor's exports continue to increase. The armaments being exported have already established their competitive edge in the world market.

Systems Management

Without satisfying the true requirements of the user, Armscor would go out of business. It works from a systems management categorisation known as 'technology space'. This space consists of three dimensions:

1. Level in the systems hierarchy

2. Phase in the life cycle

3. Type of system

The level of the systems hierarchy can be simplified by dividing it into eight levels, each with integrated elements. These levels range from the basic material through the components, sub-systems and product (say, a gun) to the product-system (gun plus support), user system (crew) to combat group and finally the operational force. Superimposed upon the product system is the life-cycle for that system. Every life-cycle phase has ever increasing activities by level in the systems hierarchy. The point to be made, without getting overtechnical, is that the scope of Armscor's systems management is well integrated and produces results. Dr. W.J. Barnard, Senior General Manager, Department of Engineering, Armscor, emphasised 'The responsibility of the engineering function, or more explicitly the ensuing systems engineering function, is to specify an optimum relationship between functional performance, cost of ownership and user-friendliness – attuned to a particular user – for the weapons systems supplied by Armscor.'

Armscor believes that it enters into a life-long commitment with the users. This becomes critical since it does not enjoy normal access to international expertise because of the existing international political climate. Nevertheless, its staff maintains credible self-reliance by covering the entire field of specialisation. This takes considerable brain-power which the corporation seems willing and able to fund.

Armscor works under the concept of a 'systems supplier', a person able to contract for systems and develop and maintain all specifications. At the contracting level, Armscor ideally prefers to contract at the product systems level (Level 5). As an example it could be a total artillery system to include gun, tractor ammunition, fire control, other mobile support and logistics. For obvious reasons, Armscor would prefer to supply all support to a weapons system. Armscor's proven armaments line gives it a substantial edge in supplying an end-user at Level 5.

Arms Embargo Tactics – Too Late?

The International Seminar on the United Nations arms embargo against South Africa held in May 1986 felt that South Africa was dependent on several key areas for its external supply of military components and therefore vulnerable to an effective arms embargo. The World Conference on Sanctions Against Racist South Africa held in June 1986, was vehement in its strong recommendations for the total enforcement of SCR 418 of 4 November 1977. Many organisations and bodies continue to urge stronger enforcement of the arms embargo. Their tactics may be too late in the face of the substantial degree of self-sufficiency which Armscor has achieved – except in the building of a complete aircraft. However, this may be short-lived in the light of the reported arrival in South Africa of nearly 50 Israeli aircraft industry engineers and technicians from the cancelled LAVI fighter project in Israel. They will be either working on the ARIEH, the scaled-down forerunner of the LAVI or the F-21 KFIR which is a copy of the Mirage 5. Armscor plans to open a plant at an existing factory in Pretoria.

Pretoria lost out on the direct sale of Class 209 submarines from West Germany, due to its Foreign Minister Hans Dietrich Genscher requesting adherence to the arms embargo. Armscor, however, did receive the submarine blueprint plans. Although South Africa initially paid R40-million for the blueprints, the state-owned Howaldtswere-Deutsche Werft A.G. (H.W.D.) in Kiel returned R21-million while R10.5 million remained with shipbuilders Ingenierkontor Luebeck (IKL). These blueprints could be the genesis of South Africa's first submarine programme if the Defence Budget 1988-89 contains large procurement funding for the S.A.N. as indicated by Helmoed-Römer Heitman, the South African Defence Force's military correspondent in the August 1987 Defence Journal.

Industry-wide connections with South Africa's Defence establishment is demonstrated by the following examples:

- Sandock-Austral, ship builders and manufacturers of armoured vehicles in South Africa, has expanded to build a $13-million dry-docking facility in Punta Arenas in Chile with Pretoria's blessing.
- Powertech's Chairman, F.J. Bell, was formerly the executive general manager of Armscor. According to the *Financial Mail* of 26 June 1987, Powertech's stock has climbed from 78 per cent to 220 per cent. Powertech is into power generation, transmission and distribution, energy measurement and control, lighting, electrical accessories and cables.

Marketing

Armscor's products are marketed extensively at international shows such as those in Santiago, Chile in 1986 and 1988. These exhibitions have proved invaluable as positive advertisements for Armscor. Prospective buyers are invited to Pretoria for extensive public relations briefings and are shown selective weapons systems in action. This is but a small part of the substantial marketing procedures of Armscor. High class, professional glossy brochures are distributed to prospective clients and those who may be instrumental in 'singing Armscor's praises'. The management realises that its in big business and seems to disappoint few in its business-like approach.

The Changing Scene

Most military experts, and the South African Defence Force, are readily aware that sustained losses of the Cheetah, G6 and armoured vehicles could not be rapidly replaced. This may be why the South Africans are cautious, however effective they may be, in their utilisation of armaments in Angola.

During the October/November 1987 Angolan conflict, the South African Defence Force's operational military tactics were predicated on the possible loss of armaments rather than intelligence information on the opponent's disposition. Lost opportunities invariably do not return. In this case there is a strong possibility that the South African's did not press their advantage. Had they done so, the total annihilation of FAPLA would have been possible. FAPLA was stopped, beaten, and then permitted to retreat. A strong follow-up by rapid pursuing troops supported by the G6 'wonder cannon', and intense air-to-ground support by attack aircraft using high-explosive bombs, and the devastating CB470 bouncing bomblets would not only have destroyed Angola's armed forces but would have given UNITA the strongest possible bargaining position in its negotiation with President Jose Eduardo dos Santos' government of Angola. This lost opportunity for Pretoria may never return. Additional Soviet equipment, the use of Cubans in direct combat roles, and the change in military strategy by Angola have been instrumental in the South African/Angolan stalemate in the early 1988 battle at Cuito Cuanavale, and the June 1988 Cuban advancement to within 12 kilometres of the Namibian border. By August 1988, the South African Air Force was completely vulnerable in Angola. This was chiefly due to the Angolan/Soviet-built MiG-23 aircraft operating in conjunction with a extensive radar network covering the whole of Angola and North Namibia. These 75 mobile radar units, with seven different types of radar, have been installed at 23 different sites. This has not gone unnoticed by Pretoria.

In July 1988 representatives from Angola, Cuba and South Africa met in the US and agreed to a set of 'essential principles' forming the groundwork for an ultimate settlement of hostilities in south-western Africa. These principles enjoined Angola and South Africa to 'co-operate' with the Secretary General of the United Nations in implementing SCR 435. (Resolution 435 of 1978 called for the withdrawal of South African troops from Namibia and free elections in order to establish majority rule and independence.) All parties continued to strengthen their bargaining positions through political and military posturing until the US Presidential elections in November. At that time, the parties rethought their strategies and tactics based on the election results.

Since all parties involved in the negotiations had a stake in south-western Africa, the outcome of the negotiations affected the national interests of each participant. Pretoria views an unacceptable government in Windhoek (Namibia's capital) as a threat to its vital interests. Access through Namibia and the Caprivi strip enhances South Africa's regional power status and is perceived as vital to Pretoria's survival. Luanda, on the other hand, is plagued by three independent politico-military forces: the Cubans, SWAPO, and UNITA, each of which demands a different strategy. With the Cubans' departure, UNITA'S chances for a successful military takeover of Angola increase considerably, a fact Luanda is deeply aware of. Ironically, Cuba, the guest that has overstayed its welcome, moved into a power broker position by default.

Against a backdrop of regional economic supremacy, South Africa is demonstrating its ability to wield political clout beyond its borders. The most visible ongoing initiative revolves around the Angola/Namibia dilemma. Ten separate discussions have been held among South Africa, Angola and Cuba, with the US mediating and the Soviet Union attending as an 'interested party'. Despite the long road ahead, progress has been made. The South Africans have pulled out of Angola. The Cubans are willing to withdraw from Angola. The 'Brazzaville Protocol' of 13 December 1988 provides for a timetable. Verification of Cuban withdrawal still remains a point of contention. A fragile ceasefire is in effect. Jonas Savimbi's National Union for the Total Independence of Angola (UNITA) and Sam Nujoma's South-West African People's Organisation (SWAPO) (both insurgent movements) have been playing their cards close to the chest. The two leaders are not about to initiate any action which might jeopardise their chances of grabbing the big prizes – in Nujoma's case, Namibia, and for Savimbi, the grand prize of Angola – or at least recognition within a coalition government.

The United Nations Transitional Administrative Group (UNTAG) supervised the elections in Namibia. This task has no doubt been eased by the adroit diplomatic moves of UN Secretary General Javier Perez de Cuellar.

Outside South Africa, Botha's much publicised meeting in Mozambique in September 1988 with President Joachim Chissano was touted as a step toward establishing formal diplomatic relations. If this comes about it will be based on political and economic realities – not any trust Chissano may have in Botha. Nevertheless, this seeming thaw is in Pretoria's favour. In addition, Botha's weekend summit in October 1988 with Zaïre's President Mobutu Sese Seko stressed South Africa's desire for *rapprochement* with its neighbours. What were not mentioned in the communique were the roles South Africa and Zaïre would play in supporting UNITA now and in the future. Both Mobutu and Botha support Savimbi and will adroitly manoeuvre in the Southern African scene for favourable circumstances for a UNITA takeover of Angola.

Grabbing an ever widening spotlight, a follow-up conference was held in Lusaka, Zambia, involving leaders of Zambia, Zaïre, Angola, Gabon and Congo. Observers from Nigeria, Ivory Coast, Mali and Mozambique also attended. These talks stressed the importance of an Angola/Namibian solution. Unofficially, sources in attendance said the conferees reiterated the existing realities in Southern Africa but were extremely wary of South Africa's motives. Nevertheless, these conferees were determined to put pressure on the Angolan Marxist Government of Jose Eduardo dos Santos to reach an accommodation with Savimbi's UNITA.

While the form that an accommodation would take is unclear, the initiative could lead to a proposition similar to the Alvor declaration of 1977, where a tripartite government was supposed to govern Angola. (The Marxist Angolan Government reneged on the proposal which led to a power grab by the existing government in Angola.) Currently a workable bipartite government of Savimbi and dos Santos seems unlikely, given the strongly different ideologies of the two men, the Cuban dimension, Soviet interests, Southern Africa's so-called frontline states' divergent views, and South Africa's fear that a Savimbi faction would quickly be purged by the Marxist Angolan Government.

Early in October 1988 while attention was pointed towards Angola, SWAPO's Sam Nujoma was mapping out a strategy for the takeover of Namibia at Franceville, a small town in south-eastern Gabon. His talks with the presidents of Angola, Gabon and Congo centred on the myriad problems SWAPO would face in the transition to governing Namibia. Nujoma's discussions centred on nationalising the mines and industry, the problems in financing his government, the flight of white technicians, the support of ANC bases and maintaining workable relations with Pretoria. The decisions he makes in these areas, if he comes to power, will quickly lead to success or failure. Should Nujoma take over Namibia, Pretoria will be looking over his shoulder.

A lingering issue, the Cuban presence in Africa, continues to receive mixed responses from African leaders; however, the general feeling throughout Southern Africa is that the Cubans must go. Previously the guarantors of Luanda's survival, the Cubans are now widely considered a destabilising force in the region. Furthermore, leaders in the region view Castro's strong rhetoric, backed by military action, as a threat to eventual stability. They are uncomfortable with his 58,000 troops armed with sophisticated Soviet weaponry. Furthermore, they are aware that Castro is making offers to employ his troops elsewhere in Africa even though a firm date has been established for Cuban withdrawal.

South Africa's hidden strategy is now becoming clear. Amid varied but connected events in Southern Africa, seemingly unconnected initiatives are strengthening Pretoria's position in the region while at the same time serving as catalysts for renewed relations among all parties in the area. The possibility of viable economic growth in the region hinges on co-operative attitudes of all parties and positive actions taken by South Africa and the frontline states toward lasting stability.

Who are the Winners and Losers in Southern Africa?

An in-depth analysis of the changing politico-military scene in Southern Africa turns up many unforeseen events that will have a strong impact on the region in the immediate future. The December 1988 'Brazzaville Protocol' was acclaimed by regional and international leaders as a positive step for peace in Southern Africa. These accords, if adhered to, will considerably lessen tensions in the region – South Africa has withdrawn from Angola and will withdraw from Namibia. Cuba will, over time, withdraw entirely from Angola and in November 1989, elections are scheduled for Namibia.

But, what is the real impact of this changing scene and who will be the winners and losers? Recent articles (Sept. '88 and Jan. '89, AFJI) have analysed the south-western African peace initiatives in some detail. The power position of each of the players will be affected in one of three ways – positively, negatively or relatively neutrally.

A lingering question now being debated among the leaders of the African National Congress (ANC) is whether the peace accords will effect their *modus operandi*. Uriah Mokeba the ANC's chief representative in Luanda, Angola, has announced that the ANC will abandon its bases in that country. He said '... things have changed. Moscow ... has deserted us.' This no doubt will be a major determinant in the ANC's decision to place more emphasis on political strategy *vice* armed struggle against South Africa (The ANC has been labelled a 'major terrorist group' by the January 1989 Pentagon *Terrorist Group Profiles*).

Despite Moscow's recent toned down rhetoric towards South Africa, Pretoria is still wary of lingering Soviet influence in the region. The first indication of a shift in Soviet thinking on South Africa came in June 1986. Gleb Starushenko, a deputy director of the Institute of African Studies in Moscow, 'urged the ANC to consider giving the white South Africans collective guarantees and group rights in a post apartheid constitution'. In addition, Pretoria's Deputy Minister of Foreign Affairs, Mr. Kobus Meiring, at an address to the Free State National Party Congress in Bloemfontein, South Africa, in early September 1988 said, 'there were signs that the USSR had come to realise that the ANC had over the years led it by the nose with falsehoods about the situation in South Africa. ...'

This supposed thaw in Soviet relations towards South Africa has not assuaged Pretoria's view of the ever present threat of the Soviets.

Moreover, President Joaquim Alberto Chissano is initiating the closing of ANC training bases in Mozambique. Pretoria's economic hand plays an important part in his decision. Mozambique is being wooed by South Africa. The Cabora Bassa project (the fourth largest hydroelectric scheme in the world) has received engineering, construction and financial support from Pretoria. This dam will generate large revenues for Mozambique. South Africa has gone on record as no longer giving military support to the insurgent Mozambican National Resistance Movement known as Renamo. Pretoria is also providing substantial economic assistance to Chissano. These changing alignments move the ANC further from establishing viable 'safe havens' to conduct guerrilla warfare against South Africa. Although the ANC headquarters is based in Lusaka, Zambia, President Kenneth Kuanda insists they keep a low profile for fear of undue retaliation by Pretoria. This leaves only Tanzania and Ethiopia, two distant countries, which accommodate ANC bases. More ANC operatives have been killed and arrested last year in South Africa than in 1987. Ostensibly, these ominous signs are moving the ANC's politburo away from a military solution to a political stratagem.

Furthermore, the ANC has recently come out with the so-called Lusaka Amendments. These proposals do not replace their Freedom Charter but rather translates the broad principles of the Charter into explicit constitutional provisions. Of ominous importance is that this is the first time since 1962 that any South African political organisation has produced a detailed blueprint and rationale for a unitary democratic constitution, according to Tom Lodge, an authoritative commentator on the ANC.

With these events in mind one can readily see changing patterns in the ANC's approach to Pretoria although their philosophy remains the same.

South Africa's retention of Walvis Bay, the only deep water harbour on the 700 mile Namibian coast, will no doubt create post-independence controversy. Pretoria is well aware of the crucial geostrategic value of this port. Although the South-West Africa People's Organisation (SWAPO) claims Walvis Bay as an integral part of Namibia it remains a part of South Africa through a quirk of European colonial history. This important South African military base with its large offshore fishing industry and the roughly 25,000 pro-South African inhabitants entrench Pretoria's position.

Although the South African Defence Force (SADF) will lose its 'combat training area' and access through the Caprivi Strip, budgetary savings on military consolidation and financial aid to Windhoek may soften Pretoria's physical withdrawal from Namibia. In addition, this will permit Pretoria to turn inward more readily and concentrate on eventual evolutionary enfranchisement of the black population. This will ward off the possible catastrophic consequences of a revolutionary schema. In Pretoria's eyes it must deal with destabilising forces which act as catalysts toward revolution, namely the growing strength of selected political parties on the right and those unions and a black consciousness umbrella movement, the United Democratic Front (UDF) on the left. Exacerbating Pretoria's dilemma is the Anglo-American Corporation's strident moves to unify the fragmented moderate left. This South African-based international mining conglomerate is intent on molding the Progressive Federal Party (PFP), the National Democratic Movement (NDM) and the Independent Party into a well-funded force bent on imposing a new liberal order in South Africa. In early February 1989 these parties merged into one, the Democratic Party. Compounding Pretoria's internal problems was the untimely stroke of South Africa's President, P.W. Botha. The end of the Angolan/Namibian conflict will enable Pretoria to direct more resources toward this end.

On 6 January 1989, President Elect George Bush made public his open support for Jonas Savimbi's National Union for the Total Independence of Angola (UNITA), in effect freeing Pretoria from supporting this Angolan-based insurgent movement against the Marxist-led government of Jose Eduardo dos Santos in Luanda. Bush's letter to Savimbi was emphatic, stating, 'Until that objective (national reconciliation) is achieved, my Administration will continue all appropriate and effective assistance to UNITA.' This pledge to Savimbi affects the military balance in Angola. Continued military material support for UNITA diminishes Luanda's chance for a knockout blow using its surrogate Cuban forces. All indications are that Savimbi can hold on until April 1991 when all Cuban forces should be withdrawn from Angola. This has ominous implications for dos Santos, who heretofore relied on sophisticated Soviet weaponry manned by Cubans. His inept army, the People's Armed Forces for the Liberation of Angola (FAPLA), is no match for a US-supplied UNITA. The Soviets may not be willing to continue to pour money and equipment down Luanda's rat hole.

Favouring increased stabilisation in Southern Africa is the minor rift in relations between Cuba's Fidel Castro and Russia's President, Mikhail Gorbachev. There are strong ideological differences over Gorbachev's *glasnost* and *perestroika*. Castro has been openly critical of Gorbachev in this regard. He has become somewhat of an embarrassment to Gorbachev, playing into the hands of Gorbachev's internal enemies. Nevertheless, Castro's Soviet-backed adventures in Africa are coming to an end.

A combination of South African emergency regulations which bars certain press releases and the recent international focus on Israel and the Palestinian leader Yasser Arafat have subsumed much negative news reporting from Pretoria while shifting international attention to the Middle East. These events in conjunction with the Assistant Secretary of State for African Affairs, Chester Crocker's astute diplomatic moves in Southern Africa have given a short term positive image to the area which reflects on South Africa.

Moreover, recent 'negative' reporting of civil rights abuses, genocide and lack of democratic jurisprudence throughout the globe has shifted the pointed attention that South Africa received prior to 1988. These events, coupled with a US/Soviet 'loose *rapprochement*', have all contributed indirectly to who is winning and who is losing in Southern Africa.

A winner is P.W. Botha's South Africa, which maintains its regional power status and gains time to implement its policies to counter the wide array of internal dissension. Sam Nujoma's SWAPO looks like a sure bet to take over the reins of government in Namibia. Chissano's Mozambique has taken its first steps towards stabilising its economy. In addition, the prospects for neutralising the insurgent movement, Renamo, look bright. Rounding out the winners is Savimbi's UNITA. Their chances of winning the guerrilla war in Angola have been increased manifold.

The neutral recipients are the BLS countries – Botswana, Lesotho and Swaziland. Their position remains relatively the same due to Pretoria's indirect grip on their economies. However, reduced conflict in the area will create an atmosphere for smoother relations with Pretoria. Also in this category is President Robert Mugabe's Zimbabwe. Although he continually denounces South Africa and its apartheid policies, he possesses little concrete leverage to counter recent unfolding events in Southern Africa. This was strongly in evidence at the 6 February 1989 Commonwealth foreign ministers' conference held in Harare, Zimbabwe. Mugabe's opening statement included harsh criticism of South Africa. Despite this criticism, Mugabe openly admitted that his own economic ills have caused a doubling of Zimbabwe's trade with South Africa. Similarly, five other Commonwealth nations attending rely substantially on South Africa's economy – Botswana, Lesotho, Swaziland, Malawi, and Zambia.

The losers are dos Santos' Marxist Government in Angola and President Oliver Tambo's ANC. Dos Santos' power will be quickly eroded after the Cuban withdrawal and the possible diminution of sophisticated Soviet weaponry. Once weakened, he will opt for a coalition government with Savimbi but if events unfold as in the above scenario, Savimbi's strong desire 'to have it all' will override any frontline state's position on a coalition government in Angola. The ANC have lost the battle but not necessarily the war. Oliver Tambo will have to adjust adroitly and rapidly in his strategy towards

South Africa. The ANC guerrilla potential is diminished considerably without bases close to South Africa. Tambo's military arm has been temporarily crippled. The question is whether he can shift into a viable political strategy to keep Pretoria on the defensive in the international community. The fight for power in Southern Africa is ongoing. Each player views his stake in the area from his perspective. Unfortunately, there will not be 'something in it for everyone' as proposed by the July 1988 agreement on a set of 'essential principles' when Angola, Cuba and South Africa met in the US forming the ground work for the ultimate settlement of hostilities in south-western Africa.

The strong need for a research and development programme for South Africa's defence establishment was vividly realised in the late 1960s. The weapons systems built in the 1940s and 1950s, would not stand up to the technologically superior armaments of the early 1970s, particularly the ultra-modern systems that were then on the drawing boards. Independence from colonial rule was sweeping the continent. The Soviets, aware that some of the new fledgling governments would have constant internal battles to stay in power, made probes, followed by some written and unwritten agreements to provide various forms of assistance. The mood of independence was sweeping across Africa – but it was a mood that was premature, since few of the countries concerned had the capacity to organise and run a modern, self-sufficient state.

Eventually the buffer states of Mozambique, Angola and Rhodesia (Zimbabwe) were no longer compatible with South Africa's view of the southern region. The external 'threat' as perceived by Pretoria was ominous not to mention the deep concern for the ever-present internal 'threat'. This, coupled with the arms embargo, reinforced the attitude of the *laager* philosophy – draw the loyal in tight, fight for survival, make a covenant and go-it-alone if necessary. Hence the heavy thrust into a weapons modernisation programme, with strong emphasis and ample resources going into research and development – the result of which is evident in today's state-of-the-art weapons systems produced by Armscor (see Appendix D).

The South African Defence Force's close working relationship with Armscor as the Defence Establishment's sole producer of armaments has created a unique working symbiotic relationship. It may have to work because there is no other choice. Nevertheless, this unencumbered, monopolistic system works. People make it work to the satisfaction of the supplier and the user with the invisible hand of

Pretoria in the background – people are the key. Such a system might not work as efficiently in different circumstances. However, for South Africa it is a functional and better way to do business.

It must be realised that the financial books of Armscor are closed to public scrutiny. The Special Defence Account and other sources of revenue are rarely revealed. So, although the Corporation is competitive in the international market for quality and price, very few, but the insiders, know the real cost of producing a weapons system. How much subsidy beyond the actual sale price is hidden under the 'legislative veil of secrecy', is anybody's guess.

Selling Its Case

The Defence Establishment, not unlike the United States and others, publishes numerous documents to sell its case. Threaded throughout these publications is a constant flow of articles on Armscor. Themes such as, 'In war our 2nd line is unseen', 'We have no choice for freedom', 'We must arm', 'Production for peace and security' and 'We can for we must' have become more subtle. Now one gets more of a 'Madison Avenue' approach, with such themes as 'Marksman Trainer ensures top score', 'The technology of space of the armaments industry', 'The nature of armaments technology', and 'Evolvement of the organisation for systems management'.

Armscor makes a considerable effort to reassure the public of the safety of its employees and that its responsiveness in caring for the flora and fauna on its test ranges is at the forefront of its decision making. They stress that the unoccupied land of these ranges, in most cases, is 'ecologically sensitive and lends itself ideally to nature conservation'. Armscor boasts that 'comprehensive programmes have been formulated to resettle game and preserve indigenous vegetation'. They cite prime examples of St. Lucia on the north Natal coast and Bredasdorp in the Southern Cape. Furthermore, they state 'Armscor's guardian role today also encourages South Africa's architectural heritage', when speaking of 'the architecturally fascinating Erasmus Castle on the site of its new headquarters outside Pretoria. ...'*

As we have seen, the thrust of Armscor's message has changed considerably from the direct approach to the more subtle type over the past ten years. Their sophisticated approach is readily apparent and there has been no discernable negative feedback from the target

---

*Armscor, a Giant in the South African Industry, undated, p.16.

audiences. However, to what extent, the projected image of Armscor impacts on the South African public and the international community is not readily apparent.

At present the prevailing mood of the Afrikaner is the dominant factor in determining which way South Africa will go. This, coupled with the mimicking of the Israeli *modus operandi* is the basis for the animosity felt towards Pretoria in Southern Africa and the United Nations. However, South Africa views its strategy as the road to survival and until such time as its perception of this reality changes, Pretoria will remain a pariah and, internal military self-sufficiency is a necessary ingredient for survival. In this scenario, as it unfolds, Armscor looms on the horizon as bigger and better thanks to large infusions of defence funding. Many defence analysts believe that South Africa can hold on like this for years, thanks to the strength of its infrastructure and the dependence and weakness of its neighbours.

The success story of Armscor is not only a product of its managerial foresight, but also of the varied political circumstances that made its planned development, starting in the 1960s and nearing its apex in the late 1980s.

South Africa would very much like to become an acceptable part of the international community. It looks upon most other nations as hypocrites as they expound ways for South Africa to ensure political franchise for all when many deny it to their own. Pretoria views its evolutionary (as opposed to revolutionary) approach to change as a solid plan that will permit the orderly flow of all South Africans into the political-economic and social mainstream of South Africa. Obviously, this is too little and too late for many. Pretoria's thinking has been conditioned by the aftermath of such concessionary moves as permitting the unionisation of mine workers and the release of the long-standing prisoner and former African National Congress (ANC) Chairman, Mr. Govan Mbeki. In the case of the mine workers, the unions have become organised elements whose efforts are directed toward political franchise and other 'subversive' moves under the tutelage of the ANC. In retrospect, Pretoria sees Mbeki's release as a big mistake. He has failed to denounce his strong Marxist ideology and has become a martyr among many blacks. Pretoria is not going to let this happen in the case of Nelson Mandela, despite Britain's Prime Minister, Margaret Thatcher's quid pro quo for a state visit to South Africa. Pretoria's attitudes have been conditioned over the years by events such as these. The relaxation of pressure as goodwill gestures, as they see it, in their planned evolutionary approach, has, more often than not, backfired. With this in mind, it is not very difficult to make predictions about the immediate future. South Africa will 'pull-in the *laager*'. The prevailing mood of Pretoria will remain. The policy of acting from a position of strength and becoming no-one's military client will be steadfastly pursued. The 'marshmallow' arms embargo and 'joint arms industry' will give Pretoria breathing room. Within this scenario, Armscor will expand. On-line weapons systems will remain state-of-the-art with the eventual breakthrough of a totally South African manufactured fighter aircraft system. The capacity, research and development within Armscor will increase, due to the expansion of its export market in weapons systems.

Appendix A

South African Defence Expenditure 1974–87

Year	% Govt Exp	% GNP	1987 Rand	1977 Rand
1974	16.4	3.2		
1975	18.5	3.2		
1976	17	5.3		
1977	18.4	4.8		R1,652
1978	16.6	4.2		R1,492
1979	16.8	4.1		R1,531
1980	16.8	3.7		R1,597
1981	17.1	4.0		R1,703
1982	16.3	3.9		R1,650
1983	15.3	3.8	R6,568	R1,611
1984	14.7	3.8	R7,031	R1,689
1985	13.7	3.9	R6,384	R1,650
1986	14.7	4.0	R6,348	(R1,559)*
1987	14.9	4.6	R6,903	(R1,696)*

* 1977 Rands approximation.

1987/8 Defence Budget: Allocation by Programme

	1987/8	1986/7
Landward Defence	35.6%	37.7%
Air Defence	37.9%	31.7%
Maritime Defence	7.2%	7.9%
Medical Service	3.1%	3.3%
Command and Control	2%	2.2%
General Support	14.2%	17.1%

1987/8 Defence Budget: Allocation By Service

	1987/8	1986/7
Army	39.2%	38.4%
Air Force	38.5%	32.1%
Navy	7.5%	8.1%
Medical Service	3.4%	4.2%
Other	11.4%	17.2%

1987/8 Defence Budget   Procurement Funds: Allocation by Service

Army	40%
Air Force	48%
Navy	6.7%
Medical Service	2.4%

Appendix B

Tracing the Origins of the
Arms Embargo

When the United Nations instituted a compulsory arms embargo against South Africa in 1977, the expectation was that the Republic would crumble, having no means of procuring armaments to defend its borders. Instead, the opposite has occurred as, forced to find a solution to the problem, South Africa established its own armaments industry. The result is that South Africa is now self-sufficient in many areas of weaponry.

Events leading up to the United Nations arms embargo against South Africa are characterised by various international and political issues. South Africa's internal policy is generally regarded in the international political arena as 'the *apartheid* policy' and is seen in the same light as colonialism, slavery and aggression.

By virtue of its charter, the United Nations may decree certain international regulations. These regulations are contained in resolutions and, depending on their nature, are considered compulsory or non-compulsory.

The two primary bodies in this regard are the General Assembly, consisting of all the member states and the Security Council, consisting of five permanent members (Britain, France, America, Russia and Canada) and ten non-permanent members.

The institution of the arms embargo can be traced to three main issues. These issues are regarded as 'serious violations of international law' and as so-called 'crimes which threaten the preservation of international peace and security'.

First, South Africa's internal '*apartheid* policy' is seen as a 'violation of human rights and as a crime against the human race'. In terms of

Chapter Seven of the United Nations Charter, *apartheid* is regarded as an 'infringement of international law'.

The second issue deals with South Africa's military build-up and is regarded as a 'basis for aggression against the RSA's neighbouring states.' In addition, the expansion of South Africa's military capabilities is seen as 'constituting a threat to international peace and security, especially to African states against *apartheid*.

The right of these states to condemn *apartheid* is directly and indirectly linked to South African military and police forces '... constitutes a potential threat to international peace and security, ... reiterates its total opposition to the policies of apartheid of the Government of the Republic of South Africa; ... calls upon all states to observe strictly the arms embargo against South Africa and to assist effectively in the implementation of this resolution'.

The last Security Council resolution (concerning the delivery of weapons to South Africa), accepted before the compulsory arms embargo of 1977, was resolution 311 of 4 February 1972.

In 1973 the nature of the resolutions in the United Nations underwent a marked change. In resolution 3151 of 14 December 1973 the Security Council was requested to 'consider urgently the situation in South Africa and the aggressive actions of the South African regime with a view to adopting effective measures, under Chapter Seven of the Charter of the United Nations, to resolve the grave situation in the area and, in particular:

- to ensure that all Governments implement fully the arms embargo against South Africa,
- to call upon the Governments concerned to refrain from importing any military supplies manufactured by, or in collaboration with South Africa,
- to call upon the Governments concerned to terminate any existing military arrangements with the South African regime'.

States were also requested to cease the exchange of military attachés.

In June 1975, a shift of emphasis with regard to the arms embargo occurred in the United Nations. The South West Africa/Namibia issue was discussed in the Security Council and a compulsory arms embargo against South Africa was requested in terms of Chapter Seven of the United Nations Charter.

This was the first time in the history of the United Nations that actions in terms of Chapter Seven of the Charter were requested. The proposal was not accepted, however, as France, Britain and the

United States voted against it (a permanent member of the Security Council can veto any proposal).

Although the proposals and actions of the General Assembly had primarily been *ad hoc* during the 1960s, they became more systematical in nature during the 1970s. These gestures were supported by such actions as international conferences. One such conference was the Lagos Conference of August 1977, regarded as an apex and influenced by South Africa's weapons build-up. The Republic's involvement in the Angolan issue of 1975/76, which is considered a direct interference in the internal affairs of a state, is seen as a further manifestation of its military capabilities. Security Council resolution 387 (1976) describes South Africa's actions as 'an act of aggression against the Angolan population and a violation of article 2(4) of the United Nations Charter'. The South West Africa/Namibia issue is the third element used to motivate the institution of the arms embargo. South Africa's administration of, and its military presence in Namibia, is regarded as unlawful in terms of resolution 2145 of 27 October 1966 and is constantly used to support the issues of apartheid and military build-up.

Attempts to institute a compulsory arms embargo against South Africa began as early as 1962, following the establishment of the UN's Special Committee against Apartheid.

The first arms embargo resolution against South Africa accepted by the Security Council was passed in 1963. This resolution, 181 of 7 August, was accepted within the framework of '... the recent arms build-up by the Government of South Africa, some of which arms are being used in furtherance of that Government's racial policies', the country's internal policy and its unwillingness to release political prisoners. Although this resolution was not compulsory, it was considered a moral obligation.

Paragraph three of the resolution states that the Security Council 'solemnly calls upon all states to cease forthwith the sale and shipment of arms, ammunition of all types of military vehicles to South Africa'.

This resolution was followed by a second one four months later (182 of 4 December). This primarily emphasised *apartheid* as a violation of human rights and South Africa's refusal to release so-called political prisoners being held under the *apartheid* law. This resolution 'solemnly calls upon all states to cease forthwith the sale and shipment of equipment and materials for the manufacture and maintenance of arms and ammunition in South Africa'.

The first resolution referring solely to the supply of weaponry was accepted in 1970. It stated, *inter alia*, that the United Nations 'convinced further that the situation resulting from the continued application of the policies of apartheid and the constant build-up of the South African Military was the primary driving force behind UN resolution 418 of 1977'. The Lagos Declaration for Action against Apartheid corresponds largely with resolution 418 and calls upon all states to, *inter alia*:

- cease any assistance or co-operation enabling South Africa to obtain nuclear capability,
- cease all sales and supplies of arms and military equipment to South Africa,
- ensure the full implementation of the arms embargo,
- urges states and international and national sporting bodies to take all appropriate steps within their jurisdiction to bring about the termination of all sporting contacts with South Africa.

By this time a compulsory arms embargo was expected, especially in the light of the Soweto riots during 1976.

The compulsory arms embargo of 1977 was to a large extent predictable. The internal situation in South Africa during 1976, especially the Soweto riots, served as a catalyst to the embargo and internationalised the political problems of South Africa.

Although the policy of *apartheid* was an annual discussion point at the General Assembly meetings and certain Security Council resolutions concerning this matter had already been adopted, real steps were only taken by the United Nations in 1976. For example, in resolutions 392 of 1976 and 417 of 1977 South Africa was condemned '... for its resort to massive violence against, and wanton killings of the African people, including school children and students, and others opposing racial discrimination. ...'

Resolutions such as these reflected the attitude towards South Africa in the United Nations at this time and provided anti-South Africa groups with the opportunity to carry out the arms embargo against the Republic. Thus, in 1977 resolution 418 was unanimously proposed and adopted in the Security Council and included the following points:

- Recognising that the military build-up and persistent acts of aggression by South Africa against the neighbouring states seriously disturb the security of those states,
- Further recognising that the existing arms embargo must be

strengthened and universally applied, without any reservations or qualifications whatsoever, in order to prevent a further aggravation of the grave situation in South Africa,

- Strongly condemning the South African Government for its acts of repression, its defiant continuance of the system of apartheid and its attacks against neighbouring independent states,
- Convinced that a mandatory arms embargo needs to be universally applied against South Africa in the first instance,
- Decided that all states shall cease forthwith any provision to South Africa of arms and related material of all types, including the sale or transfer of weapons and ammunition, military vehicles and eqipment, paramilitary police equipment and spare parts for the aforementioned, and shall cease as well the provision of all types of equipment and supplies, and grants of licencing and arrangements, for the manufacture of maintenance of the aforementioned,
- Calls on all States to review, having regard to the objectives of this resolution, all existing contractual arrangements with and licences granted to South Africa relating to the manufacture and maintenance of arms, ammunition of all types and military equipment and vehicles, with a view to terminating them.

On close analysis of the resolution it appears that:

- the political situation in South Africa during 1976 was the mechanism used by anti-South African groups to implement the arms embargo.
- the resolution is phrased very generally, although revisions are possible.
- the resolution shows well-planned actions against South Africa not previously foretold or expected.

Resolution 418 was adopted by the Security Council within the framework of Chapter VII of the UN Charter, thus compelling all states to comply with it. In support of resolution 418, resolution 421 was adopted in December 1977. In accordance with this resolution a committee was formed, made up of all the members of the Security Council, and appointed to monitor the implementation of resolution 418. This committee was referred to as Security Council Committee 421.

Security Council Committee 421

The functions of this committee are clearly set out in resolution 421 and include the following:

- To examine the report on the progress of the implementation of resolution 418 which will be submitted by the Secretary-General;
- To study ways and means by which the mandatory arms embargo could be made more effective against South Africa and to make recommendations to the Council;
- To seek from all states further information regarding the action taken by them concerning the effective implementation of the provisions laid down in resolution 418;
- Calls upon all states to co-operate fully with the committee in regard to the fulfilment of its tasks concerning the effective implementation of the provisions of resolution 418 of 1977 and to supply such information as may be sought by the Committee in pursuance of the present solution.

Problems Encountered with the Implementation of Resolution 418

In a report compiled by the Security Council Committee 421, three main problem areas regarding the implementation of resolution 418 were identified:

- Contraventions of the arms embargo.
- The committee determined that dual purpose items and embargoed goods are delivered to South Africa via a third party. It points out that state legislation does not forbid the delivery of weaponry to a third party whilst the final destination of the goods is unknown.
- The committee further alleges that South Africa receives, to a large extent, weaponry and especially components therefore from third parties. It questions South Africa's ability to manufacture the components itself.
- Legislation adopted by states.
  Legislation with regard to the arms embargo was adopted by more than 118 states. However, the committee found that in most cases the legislation was vague, ambiguous and unsatisfactory and that stricter measures need to be taken.
- Wording of Resolution 418.
  The wording of Resolution 418 is presently one of the biggest problem areas for Security Council Committee 421. Differences in interpretation within the international community over the

intention and meaning of 'arms and related material' lead to large scale confusion.

One committee member states that '... the term "related material" included any commodity or know-how in the form of designs, drawings or documentation which was likely to increase South Africa's military or paramilitary capacity. Thus, the embargo should include, *inter alia*, the transfer of equipment and technology for all kinds of aircraft, including those which were exported ostensibly for civilian purposes, telecommunication, diesel and petrol engines of all kinds and some types of special steel alloys.'

It was proposed that a list be compiled in which all items falling within the 'arms and related material' category be specified, so that contravenors of the embargo have no excuse. Because of the fact that the wording does not define weapons *per se*, the committee considers it possible for South Africa to import certain strategically important and non-military items; to import items originally intended for private use but which are actually used for military purposes and lastly, private companies are able to provide items of strategic military value to the weapons industry in South Africa.

It seems clear that the committee is endeavouring to define 'arms and related material', determine which items are of military and which are of non-military value, define 'dual-purpose' items and determine the final destination of goods.

The wording of paragraph three of Resolution 418 also poses a problem and gives rise to one of the biggest loopholes in that resolution. It describes what is meant by licencing, contractual agreements and related questions.

The committee's report states: 'The word "review" in paragraph three of Resolution 418 has been considered to be lacking in precision. Some states have interpreted the provision regarding the termination of licences as either conditional or voluntary.' It further states that steps must be taken to stop all existing loopholes in the resolution.

Recommendations made by Security Council Committee 421

The Committee makes use of two primary sources to monitor information regarding contravention of Resolution 418. These sources are the Centre against Apartheid and Abdul Minty, Director of the World Campaign Against Military and Nuclear Collaboration with South Africa.

However, the only real monitoring function which the Security Council Committee has performed so far, is to compile a report regarding ways to improve the application of Resolution 418.

The Chairman of the Committee summed up the aim of the report and the recommendations made as follows:

'The recommendations submitted by the Committee for the consideration of the Security Council are designed to put an end to the "loopholes" and to illegal acts of "sanction-breaking". They aim at reinforcing the embargo, making it more comprehensive and creating a tangible structure for its implementation. Among other things, the recommendations deal with the questions of "dual-purpose" equipment, spare parts for military items in the possession of South Africa, the transfer of technology and licences for the manufacture of arms in South Africa, nuclear collaboration with South Africa, enforcement measures by States in the implementation of the embargo, imports of weapons from South Africa and so on.'

This report has not yet been approved by the Security Council, however.

Strengthening of the Arms Embargo Resolution 558 (1984)

In 1984, at the request of The Netherlands, the Security Council adopted a resolution in which members and non-members of the UN were requested not to import weapons manufactured by South Africa. The Netherlands delegation alleges that such an embargo will strengthen Resolution 418, seeing that South Africa's ability to produce weapons presently undermines it. The Netherlands' representative, Van der Stoel, said in motivation of Resolution 558: '... The South African Government does not conceal the fact that it seeks to become self-sufficient in military equipment and to create a broad-based defence industry which is capable of manufacturing everything the South African Defence Force requires. On the contrary, it has occasionally boasted of its progress in this regard. It is becoming clear, therefore, that South Africa's intensified efforts to build up its capacity to manufacture armaments undermines the effectiveness of the mandatory arms embargo against that country. ... It is our firm belief, therefore, that the international community must keep up the pressure on the South African Government until it shows signs of readiness to initiate a process of fundamental reforms, leading to the elimination of *apartheid*.'

'... The draft resolution before us requests all states to refrain from imports of arms, ammunition of all types and military vehicles produced in South Africa, and to strictly apply all its provisions. Finally, it requests the Secretary-General to report on its implementation to the Security Council Committee established by resolution 421 (1977) before 31 December 1985.'

Resolution 558 was unanimously adopted by the Security Council on 13 December 1984.

Resolution 558 is not mandatory and only places a moral duty on states. The adoption of this resolution as an extension of the arms embargo and can be regarded as recognition of South Africa's ability to manufacture and maintain weaponry on the one hand, and as an indication of anti-RSA groupings' dedication to implement a comprehensive and watertight embargo against arms embargo on the other.*

Appendix C

Armaments Development and Production Act No. 57 of 1968

ARMAMENTS DEVELOPMENT AND PRODUCTION ACT NO. 57 OF 1968

[ASSENTED TO 10 JUNE, 1968]
[DATE OF COMMENCEMENT: 19 JUNE, 1968]

(*Afrikaans text signed by the State President*)

as amended by

Armaments Development and Production Amendment Act,
No. 65 of 1972
Armaments Development and Production Amendment Act,
No. 20 of 1977
Armaments Development and Production Amendment Act,
No. 5 of 1978
Finance Act, No. 21 of 1980
[with effect from 31 March, 1980–see title FINANCE]
Armaments Development and Production Amendment Act,
No. 86 of 1980
Armaments Development and Production Amendment Act,
No. 56 of 1982

ACT

To establish a corporation for the development and production of armaments; to empower the Minister of Defence to prohibit or control

the export, marketing, import, conveyance through the Republic, development and manufacture of armaments; to repeal the Armaments Act, 1964; to provide for other incidental matters.

[Long title substituted by s. 9 of Act No. 20 of 1977 and by s. 5 of Act No. 56 of 1982.]

1. **Definitions.**–In this Act, unless the context otherwise indicates–

"**armaments**" includes any vessels, vehicles, aircraft, bombs, ammunition or weapons, or any substance, material, raw material, components, equipment system, articles or technique of whatever nature capable of being used in the development, manufacture or maintenance of armaments or for defence purposes or other purposes determined by the Minister with the concurrence of the Minister of Economic Affairs;

[Definition of "armaments" substituted by s. 1 (*a*) of Act No. 20 1977 and by s. 1 (*a*) of Act No. 86 of 1980.]

"**Armaments Board**" means the Armaments Board established under the Armaments Act, 1964;

"**board**" means the board of directors referred to in section 5;

"**company**" means any association of persons, whether incorporated or unincorporated;

"**corporation**" means the Armaments Corporation of South Africa, Limited, established by section 2;

[Definition of "corporation" substituted by s. 1 (*b*) of Act No. 20 of 1977.]

"**director**" means a director appointed under section 5;

"**employee**" means a person in the employment of the corporation or a subsidiary company, and in addition–

(*a*) for the purposes of section 8C (1) in so far as it relates to representations concerning the termination of employment of a person who, as a result of such termination of employment ceased to be so in employment, such person;

(*b*) for the purposes of section 4A–

(i) a person working for or who is in the employment of a person working for the corporation or a subsidiary company;

(ii) ......
[Definition of "employee" inserted by s. 1 (*a*) of Act No. 65 of 1972. Sub-para. (ii) deleted by s. 1 (*c*) of Act No. 20 of 1977.]

"employees' association" means an organization of employees which, in terms of the provisions of this Act, is recognized by the coporation as an employees' association;
[Definition of "employees' association" inserted by s. 1 (*a*) of Act No. 65 of 1972.]

"employer" means the corporation or a subsidiary company;
[Definition of "employer" inserted by s. 1 (*a*) of Act No. 65 of 1972.]

"import" in relation to armaments, includes the bringing thereof into the Republic at any harbour or airport or other place on board any vessel or aircraft or other means of conveyance, irrespective of whether or not the armaments are off-loaded from such vessel or aircraft or other means of conveyance for convey-ance through the Republic to any place outside the Republic or for any other purpose, or are intended to be so off-loaded; and **"import"**, when used as a verb, shall have a corresponding meaning;
[Definition of "import" inserted by s. 1 of Act No. 56 of 1982.]

"manufacture", in relation to armaments, includes the assembly thereof; and **"manufacture"**, when used as a verb, shall have a corresponding meaning;
[Definition of "manufacture" inserted by s. 1 of Act No. 56 of 1982.]

"marketing" includes any negotiations, offer, tender, advertising or giving of information relating to armaments and the providing of trade information; and **"market"** when used as a verb shall be construed accordingly;
[Definition of "marketing" inserted by s. 1 (*b*) of Act No. 86 of 1980.]

"Minister" means the Minister of Defence;

"non-white person" means a person who is not a white person;
[Definition of "non-white person" inserted by s. 1 (*b*) of Act No. 65 of 1972.]

"prescribe" means prescribe by regulation and **"prescribed"** shall have a corresponding meaning;
[Definition of "prescribe" inserted by s. 1 (*b*) of Act No. 65 of 1972.]

"**regulations**" means regulations made under this Act;

"**Republic**" includes the territory of South-West Africa;

"**strike**" means any one or more of the following acts or omissions by any number of employees–

(*a*)   the refusal or failure by them to continue to work (irrespective of whether the discontinuance is complete or partial) or to resume their work or to comply with the terms or conditions of their employment, or the retardation by them of the progress of work, or the obstruction by them of work; or

(*b*)   the breach or unlawful termination by them of their contracts of employment; if–

(i) such an act or omission occurs in the pursuance of any collusion, agreement or understanding, whether expressed or not, among them; and

(ii) the purpose of such an act or omission is to induce or compel the corporation or a subsidiary company–

(*aa*)   to agree to or to comply with any demands or proposals concerning terms or conditions of employment or other matters made by or on behalf of the said employees or any of them, or by or on behalf of any other persons who are or have been employed; or

(*bb*)   to refrain from giving effect to any intention to change any terms or conditions of employment, or, if such a change has been made, to restore the terms or conditions to those which existed before the change was made; or

(*cc*)   to employ or to suspend or terminate the employment of any person;

[Definition of "strike" inserted by s. 1 (*c*) of Act No. 65 of 1972.]

"**subsidiary company**" means–

(*a*)   a company of which all the issued shares are held by the corporation and its nominees or by such nominees; or

(b)   a company of which all the issued shares are held by a subsidiary company referred to in paragraph (a) and its nominees or by such nominees;

[Definition of "subsidiary company" inserted by s. 1 (c) of Act No. 65 of 1972.]

"**technique**" includes any expertise or knowledge, however depicted or recorded;

[Definition of "technique" inserted by s. 1 (c) of Act No. 86 of 1980.]

"**white person**" means a person who in appearance obviously is, or who is generally accepted as a white person, but does not include a person, who, although in appearance obviously a white person, is generally accepted as a non-white person.

[Definition of "white person" inserted by s. 1 (d) of Act No. 65 of 1972.]

"**this Act**" includes the regulations.

2.   Establishment of Armaments Development and Production Corporation of South Africa, Limited.–(1) As from a date to be fixed by the State President by proclamation in the *Gazette*, there shall be established a body to be known as the Armaments Development and Production Corporation of South Africa, Limited, which shall be a body corporate, capable of suing and being sued in its corporate name and of performing, subject to the provisions of this Act, all such acts as are necessary for or incidental to the carrying out of its objects, the exercise of its powers and the performance of its functions.

(2) The Registrar of Companies shall enter the name of the corporation in his registers on the date so fixed.

(3) (a) As from the commencement of the Armaments Development and Production Amendment Act, 1977, the corporation established by subsection (1) shall be known as the Armaments Corporation of South Africa, Limited.

(b) The Registrar of Companies shall at such commencement record such change of name in his register.

[Sub-s. (3) added by s. 2 of Act No. 20 of 1977.]

(4) Any reference in any other law or elsewhere to the Armaments Development and Production Corporation of South Africa, Limited, or to the Armaments Board shall be construed

as a reference to the Armaments Corporation of South Africa, Limited.

[Sub-s. (4) added by s. 2 of Act No. 20 of 1977.]

2A. Vesting of assets, rights, liabilities and obligations of Armaments Board in corporation.–(1) As from the date of commencement of the Armaments Development and Production Amendment Act, 1977–

> (*a*) all the assets, rights, liabilities and obligations of the Armaments Board shall vest in the corporation; and

> (*b*) anything done prior to that date by the Armaments Board in terms of the provisions of the Armaments Act, 1964 (Act No. 37 of 1964), shall be deemed to have been done by the corporation in terms of the provisions of this Act.

(2) The registrar of deeds concerned shall, as soon as practicable after the date mentioned in subsection (1), make such entries or endorsements in or on any relevant register, title deed or other document in his office or submitted to him as he may deem necessary in order to give effect to the provisions of subsection (1) (*a*), and no transfer duty, stamp duty, office fee or other charge shall be payable in respect of any vesting in terms of the said subsection (1) (*a*) or in respect of any such entry or endorsement.

[S. 2A inserted by s. 3 of Act No. 20 of 1977.]

2B. Vesting of certain property in corporation.–As from the date of commencement of the Armaments Development and Production Amendment Act, 1978, all the rights and obligations of the State and of the Council for Scientific and Industrial Research mentioned in section 4A*ter* (1), in respect of all the movable property that was immediately prior to that date used exclusively in connection with the work performed by the officers and employees referred to in that section, shall, without any liability to pay compensation, vest in the corporation.

[S. 2B inserted by s. 1 of Act No. 5 of 1978.]

2C. Vesting of certain State property in corporation.–As from the date of commencement of the Armaments Development and Production Amendment Act, 1978, all movable State property that was immediately prior to that date used exclusively for the purposes of the Atlas Aircraft Corporation of South Africa (Proprietory)

Limited, shall, without any liability to pay compensation, vest in the corporation.

[S. 2C inserted by s. 1 of Act No. 5 of 1978.]

3. Objects and general powers of corporation.–(1) The objects of the corporation shall be to meet as effectively and economically as may be feasible the armaments requirements of the Republic, as determined by the Minister, including armaments required for export and firearms, ammunition or pyrotechnical products required for supply to members of the public.

[Sub-s. (1) substituted by s. 4(a) of Act No. 20 of 1977.]

(2) For the attainment of its objects the corporation shall, in addition to any other powers vested in it by this Act, have power–

(*a*) to take over and, if necessary, to expand any undertaking of the Armaments Board for the manufacture of armaments;

(*b*) to take over any direct or indirect financial interests of the Armaments Board in any undertaking connected with the manufacture of armaments;

(*c*) to take over all assets, liabilities, rights and obligations which, in terms of the provisions of section 5 (1) of the Armaments Act, 1964 (Act No. 87 of 1964), had devolved upon the Armaments Board;

(*d*) to establish, with the approval of the Minister granted in consultation with the Minister of Economic Affairs, undertakings for the performance or promotion of the activities referred to in paragraph (*l*), or to have part in the establishment thereof, or to take over such undertakings or to acquire a share therein;

(*e*) with the approval of the Minister granted in consultation with the Minister of Economic Affairs, to promote or assist in the promotion of companies for the performance or the promotion of the activities referred to in paragraph (*l*), the Republic or elsewhere;

(*f*) with the approval of the Minister granted in consultation with the Minister of Economic Affairs, to lend or advance money to a person or company engaged in any undertaking for the performance or promotion of the activities referred to in paragraph (*l*), to acquire an interest in, or to provide, or by underwriting or otherwise to assist in the subscription of, capital for such company or to finance it or to facilitate, promote, guide or assist the financing thereof: Provided that if such act is performed in respect of a subsidiary company, the approval of the Minister is not required;

(*f*A)   to erect, construct or maintain or enter into contracts for the erection, construction or maintenance of any buildings, structures or other works required by the corporation for the performance of its functions or by the State for such purposes as the Minister may determine;
[Para. (*f*A) inserted by s. 4 (*b*) of Act No. 20 of 1977.]

(*f*B)   to obtain or establish facilities in order to achieve the objects of this Act;
[Para. (*f*B) inserted by s. 4 (*b*) of Act No. 20 of 1977.]

(*g*)   to hold, manage, develop, let or hire, or buy, subscribe for or otherwise acquire, or sell or otherwise dispose of, or hypothecate or otherwise deal in, immovable or movable property of whatever kind, including stocks, shares, bonds, debentures and securities of, and any interest in, any company, and where necessary, to act as trustee for debenture holders;

(*h*)   to make, draw, accept or endorse negotiable instruments;

(*i*)   to guarantee any undertaking given in relation to the financing of any person or company or the performance of any contract by any person or company;

(*j*)   to act as the manager or secretary of any company, and to appoint any person to act on behalf of the corporation as a director of or in any other capacity in relation to any company, and to act as the agent or representative of other companies, whether carrying on business in the Republic or elsewhere;

(*k*)   to procure the registration of the corporation in any country or territory;

(*k*A)   to undertake or cause to be undertaken in the Republic or elsewhere any investigation or research in connection with the manufacture, maintenance, testing, inspection or development of armaments;

[Para. (*k*A) inserted by s. 4 (*c*) of Act No. 20 of 1977.]

(*k*B)   to promote and co-ordinate the development, manufacture, standardization, maintenance, acquisition or supply of armaments by collaborating with, or assisting or rendering services to, or utilizing the services of, any person, body or institution or any department of State, or by taking such other steps as the corporation may consider necessary;

[Para. (*k*B) inserted by s. 4 (*c*) of Act No. 20 of 1977.]

(*l*)   to develop, manufacture, service, repair and maintain, on its own account or as the representative of any other person to buy, sell, import or export and, through advertising or otherwise, to promote the sale of, armaments, including armaments required for export and firearms, ammunition or pyrotechnical products required for supply to members of the public;

[Para. (*l*) substituted by s. 2 (*a*) of Act No. 86 of 1980.]

(*l* A)   to exercise control over the development, manufacture, acquisition, supply, export or marketing of armaments;

[Para. (*l* A) inserted by s. 4 (*d*) of Act No. 20 of 1977 and substituted by s. 2 (*b*) of Act No. 86 of 1980.]

(*l* B)   in the Republic or elsewhere, to acquire, modify, test, inspect, lease, dispose of, lend or let armaments;

[Para. (*l* B) inserted by s. 4 (*d*) of Act No. 20 of 1977.]

(*l* C)   to enter into contracts with persons in the Republic or elsewhere for the manufacture, modification, maintenance, testing or inspection of armaments;

[Para. (*l* C) inserted by s. 4 (*d*) of Act No. 20 of 1977.]

(*l* D)   to render to any person, company, body established by or in terms of any law, department of State or provincial administration such services as may from time to time be determined by the Minister who shall, if the services are required by any person, company or any such body, act with the concurrence of the Minister of Economic Affairs;

[Para. (*l* D) inserted by s. 4 (*d*) of Act No. 20 of 1977.]

(*l* E)   on behalf of any person, company, body established by or in terms of any law, department of State or provincial administration, to enter into contracts with persons in the Republic or elsewhere for the supply or rendering of armaments or services, which services shall be determined as in the case of services mentioned in paragraph (*l* D);

[Para. (*l* E) inserted by s. 4 (*d*) of Act No. 20 of 1977.]

(*l* F)   to make such arrangements as the Minister may with the concurrence of the Minister of Economic Affairs consider necessary for the stock-piling of strategic raw materials, materials and components for the manufacture of armaments;

[Para. (*l* F) inserted by s. 4 (*d*) of Act No. 20 of 1977.]

(*l* G)   to collaborate with any educational, scientific or other body or institution in connection with the provision of instruction for or the training of persons for professional or technical service or as skilled artisans in the manufacture, maintenance or development of armaments, and to provide on such conditions as it may deem fit financial or other assistance to such persons in order to enable them to receive such instruction or undergo such training;

[Para. (*l* G) inserted by s. 4 (*d*) of Act No. 20 of 1977.]

(*m*)   to apply for, buy or otherwise acquire patents, licences, concessions, rights of manufacture or the like, conferring a right to the use of any information or process, the use of which in the opinion of the corporation is necessary for the attainment of any of its objects, and to use, exercise, develop, grant licences in respect of or otherwise derive benefit from property, rights or information thus acquired;

(*m*A)   to advise the Minister on any matter relating to armaments which he may refer to the corporation or as to which the corporation may consider it to be necessary to advise the Minister;

[Para. (*m*A) inserted by s. 4 (*e*) of Act No. 20 of 1977.]

(*n*)   to engage employees;

(*o*) to establish an internal insurance fund for the insurance, on the conditions approved of by the Minister in consultation with the Minister of Finance, of the assets of the corporation or a subsidiary company;

and the corporation shall, generally, have power to enter into any contract or perform any act, whether in the Republic or elsewhere, which may be necessary for or incidental or conducive to the attainment of any of the objects of the corporation, or which is calculated directly or indirectly to enhance the value of the services which the corporation may render in respect of any of the activities referred to in paragraph (*l*), or which the Minister may from time to time determine.

[S. 3 substituted by s. 2 of Act No. 65 of 1972.]

3A. Transfer of ownership.–The ownership and other real rights registered in favour of the State in respect of the land upon which the undertakings and assets referred to in paragraphs (*a*) and (*c*) of section 3 (2) are situated, or in respect of any undivided share in such land, may, notwithstanding anything to the contrary contained in any law, be transferred directly from the State to the corporation or a subsidiary company.

[S. 3A inserted by s. 3 of Act No. 65 of 1972.]

4. Manner in which corporation shall exercise its powers.–In exercising its powers the corporation shall–

(*a*) deal with any application, proposal or other matter with a view to meeting the armaments requirements of the Republic as effectively and economically as may be feasible, having regard to the strategic value of particular armaments;

(*b*) carefully review all matters relating to raw materials necessary for the development or production of armaments, to the labour supply available for such development or production, to the rates of wages proposed to be paid and to the armaments requirements of the Republic, including armaments required for export and firearms or ammunition required for supply to members of the public, having regard to the markets available for the disposal of armaments.

4A. Powers of corporation in respect of employees.–The corporation may–

(*a*) employ the employees referred to in paragraph (*n*) of section 3 (2) on such conditions, including remuneration and the furnishing of benefits, as it may deem fit and may discharge such employees;

(*b*) on such conditions and with such security as it may deem fit–

(i) lend money to any employee; or

(ii) provide collateral security, including guarantees, to a building society in respect of a loan granted to any employee by such building society,

to enable such employee to acquire land for the erection of a dwelling house, intended for occupation by an employee, thereon, or to enable such employee to acquire, erect, improve or enlarge such a dwelling house, and may secure money which it so lends to an employee by the registration of a bond in favour of itself and may cede to renounce a bond so registered;

(*c*) build, or cause to be built, or buy or hire dwelling houses for occupation by employees and may sell or let such houses to employees or otherwise alienate, let or deal with such houses;

(*d*) build, or cause to be built, or buy or hire flat buildings and may sell or let such flat buildings or sections thereof to employees or otherwise alienate, let or deal with such flat buildings;

(*e*) establish, institute, erect or carry on medical schemes, sports and recreational societies, social clubs, social and health services, restaurants, hostels, bursary schemes for purposes of study or other similar undertakings or schemes which in its opinion are or may be beneficial to employees; and

(*f*) establish a pension scheme or a pension fund for employees and make such rules in connection therewith as it may deem fit.

[S. 4A inserted by s. 4 of Act No. 65 of 1972.]

4A*bis.* **Staff of Armaments Board to become employees of corporation.**–(1) As from the date of commencement of the Armaments Development and Production Amendment Act, 1977, the service, with the Armaments Board, of every person who is on that date in the service of the Armaments Board shall terminate and he shall become an employee of the corporation.

(2) Save in pursuance of disciplinary measures applied by the corporation, the salary or scale of salary of any person who so becomes an employee of the corporation shall not be reduced without his consent.

(3) Any leave which may have accrued in favour of any such person before he so became an employee of the corporation, shall be deemed to have accrued in his favour by virtue of service with the corporation.

(4) Subject to the provisions of subsections (2) and (3), the corporation may determine the renumeration, furnishing of benefits and other conditions of service of persons who become employees of the corporation in terms of subsection (1), as it may deem fit.

[S. 4A*bis* inserted by s. 5 of Act No. 20 of 1977.]

4A*ter.* **Certain officers and employees to become employees of corporation.**–(1) Any person who immediately prior to the date of commencement of the Armaments Development and Production Amendment Act, 1978, was an officer or employee of the Council for Scientific and Industrial Research mentioned in section 2 of the Scientific Research Council Act, 1962 (Act 32 of 1962), and was seconded to the service of the corporation or a subsidiary company, shall as from that date become an employee of the corporation.

(2) Save in pursuance of disciplinary measures applied by the corporation, the salary of any person who so becomes an employee of the corporation shall not be reduced without his consent.

(3) Any leave which may have accrued in favour of any such person before he so became an employee of the corporation, shall be deemed to have accrued in his favour by virtue of service with the corporation.

(4) Subject to the provisions of subsections (2) and (3), the corporation may determine the remuneration, furnishing of benefits

and other conditions of service of persons who become employees of the corporation in terms of subsection (1), as it may deem fit.

[S. 4A*ter* inserted by s. 2 of Act No. 5 of 1978.]

4B. Powers of corporation in connection with safeguarding of property and premises.–(1) The corporation may take or cause to be taken such measures as it considers necessary for the efficient protection, defence or safeguarding of property belonging to or under the control of the corporation or a subsidiary company or of any premises upon which any activity of the corporation or a subsidiary company is being performed, and shall in connection with any measures so taken cause such notices to be published or such warnings to be erected as it may in each particular case consider necessary.

(2) Any person authorised thereto in writing by the corporation may–

(*a*) search any person who or vehicle which is upon premises referred to in subsection (1) and open and examine any receptacle or parcel which is in the possession of such person or upon such vehicle;

(*b*) seize any object which, other than for the purposes of the performance of the functions of the corporation or a subsidiary company, is in possession of a person referred to in paragraph (*a*) or upon a vehicle so referred to and which–

(i) belongs to the corporation or a subsidiary company or is under the control of the corporation or a subsidiary company; or

(ii) constitutes a threat to the safety of the property of the corporation or a subsidiary company or the safety of property under the control of the corporation or a subsidiary company; and

(*c*) arrest any person who is in possession of an object referred to in paragraph (*b*).

(3) any person who, upon premises referred to in subsection (1), is, without lawful cause, in possession of an object referred to in subsection (2) (*b*), shall be guilty of an offence and liable on conviction to a fine not exceeding five thousand rand or to imprisonment for a period not exceeding ten years, or to both such fine and such imprisonment.

(4) The corporation or a subsidiary company or any agent of the corporation or any person employed by the corporation or a subsidiary company shall not be liable for any loss or damage resulting from any bodily injury, loss of life or loss of or damage to property or livestock caused by or arising out of or in connection with any measures taken or works erected for the safeguarding, defence or protection of property referred to in subsection (1) or of premises so referred to.

[S. 4B inserted by s. 4 of Act No. 65 of 1972.]

4C. **Powers of Minister in relation to export, marketing, import, conveyance in transit, development and manufacture of armaments.**– (1) The Minister may, whenever he deems it necessary or expedient for the security of the Republic or in the public interest–

   (*a*) by notice in the *Gazette* or by notice in writing to a particular person prescribe that no armaments of a specified class or kind or no armaments other than armaments of a specified class or kind–

   (i) shall be exported from the Republic;

   (ii) shall be exported from the Republic, except under the authority of and in accordance with the conditions stated in a permit issued by him or by a person authorised by him;

   (iii) shall be marketed within or outside the Republic;

   (iv) shall be marketed within or outside the Republic, except under the authority of and in accordance with the conditions stated in a permit issued by him or by a person authorized by him;

   (v) shall be imported into the Republic, or conveyed through the Republic from any place outside the Republic to any other such place;

   (vi) shall be imported into the Republic, or conveyed through the Republic from any place outside the Republic to any other such place, except under the authority of and in accordance with the conditions stated in a permit issued by him or by a person authorised by him; or

   (vii) shall be developed or manufactured within the

Republic, except under the authority of and in accordance with the conditions stated in a permit issued by him or by a person authorised by him;

(b) by notice in the *Gazette* or by notice in writing to the owner of armaments intended for export or marketing but the export or maketing of which is prohibited in terms of paragraph (a), direct such owner–

(i) to deliver such armaments to the Minister or to a person designated by him; or

(ii) to market such armaments through the agency of the Minister or of a person designated by him,

on such conditions as the Minister may deem fit, and the Minister may in his discretion dispose of armaments delivered in terms of subparagraph (i).

(2) For the purposes of subsection (1) armaments may be classified also according to the source or origin or the intermediate or final destination thereof or according to the channels along which or manner in which they are exported, marketed, imported or conveyed in transit or according to the manner in which or material from which they are developed or manufactured or according to the purposes for which they are intended to be used.

(3) A permit issued under subsection (1) may prescribe the quantity or value of armaments which may be exported, marketed, imported, conveyed in transit, developed or manufactured thereunder, the price at which, the period within which, the port through or from which, the country or territory from or to which, the route along which and the manner in which the armaments in question may be exported, marketed, imported, conveyed in transit, developed or manufactured, and such other conditions, of whatever nature, as the Minister may direct.

(4) The Minister may cancel, amend or suspend any permit issued under subsection (1) if he is satisified that any condition of the permit has not been complied with, or if the holder of the permit has been convicted of an offence under this Act, or if the Minister deems it necessary or expedient for the security of the Republic or in the public interest.

(5) The Minister may by like notice withdraw or amend any notice issued under subsection (1).

(6) If a notice published in the *Gazette* under subsection (1) (*a*) (vii) prohibits the development or manufacture in the Republic without a permit of armaments which on the date on which the prohibition comes into operation in terms of such notice, are lawfully developed or manufactured in the Republic by any person other than the corporation, such person shall during the period of six months after the said date be deemed to be the holder of a permit issued to him under the said subsection for the development or manufacture of the armaments which on that day he may lawfully develop or manufacture.
[S. 4C inserted by s. 3 of Act No. 86 of 1980 and substituted by s. 2 of Act No. 56 of 1982.]

4D. Furnishing of information to Minister.–The Minister or any person authorized by him may in writing direct any person who exports, markets, develops or manufactures armaments or trades in any armaments or in the course of his business or trade or otherwise handles or disposes of any armaments, to furnish the Minister within a specified period with any information at his disposal in relation to the export, marketing, development, manufacture, supply or storage of the armaments in question.
[S. 4D inserted by s. 3 of Act No. 86 of 1980.]

4E. Offences in connection with export, marketing, import, conveyance in transit, development and manufacture of armaments.–Any person who–

(*a*) exports, markets, imports, conveys through the Republic, develops or manufactures armaments in contravention of the provisions of a notice issued under section 4C (1) (*a*); or

(*b*) fails to comply with a condition stated in a permit issued under section 4C (1) (*a*); or

(*c*) fails to comply with a direction issued under section 4C (1) (*b*) or 4D; or

(*d*) furnishes any false information in complying with a direction referred to in section 4D,

shall be guilty of an offence and liable on conviction to a fine not exceeding ten thousand rand or to imprisonment for a period not exceeding ten years or to both such fine and such imprisonment.
[S. 4E inserted by s. 3 of Act No. 86 of 1980 and substituted by s. 3 of Act No. 56 of 1982.]

4F.   Inspection of armaments factories.–(1) Any employee of the corporation, or any other person, authorized thereto in writing by the Minister may at any time enter any factory or premises where armaments are developed or manufactured under a permit issued in terms of section 4C (1) (*a*) (vii), and there carry out such inspection as he may deem necessary to ascertain whether the conditions of the permit have been or are being complied with.

(2) Any person who exercises any power in terms of this section shall, at the request of any person affected by the exercise of that power, identify himself and produce the inspection authority in writing furnished to him in accordance with subsection (1).

(3) Any person who hinders or obstructs an employee or other person authorized as contemplated in subsection (1) in the exercise of the powers conferred upon him by that subsection, and any person who falsely represents himself to be authorized as contemplated in that subsection, shall be guilty of an offence and liable on conviction to a fine not exceeding one thousand rand or to imprisonment for a period not exceeding six months or to both such fine and such imprisonment.

[S. 4F inserted by s. 4 of Act No. 56 of 1982.]

5.   Board of directors.–(1) The affairs of the corporation shall, subject to the provisions of this Act, be managed and controlled by a board of directors.

[Sub-s. (1) substituted by s. 5 of Act No. 65 of 1972.]

(2) The board shall consist of not less than seven and not more than twelve directors to be appointed by the State President.

[Sub-s. (2) substituted by s. 3 of Act No. 5 of 1978.]

(3) No decision taken by the board or act performed under the authority of the board shall be invalid merely by reason of a vacancy on the board or of the fact that any person not entitled to sit as a director sat as a director at the time the decision was taken or the act was authorised, if the decision was taken or the act was authorised by the required majority of directors present at the time, who were entitled to sit as directors.

(4) The directors shall hold office for such period, not exceeding three years, as the State President may determine at the time of

appointment, but shall be eligible for re-appointment: Provided that if in his opinion there are good reasons for doing so, the State President may at any time terminate the period of office of any director.

(5) A director designated by the State President as chairman, or, in his absence, a director so designated as deputy chairman, shall preside at any meeting of the board: Provided that if both the chairman and they deputy chairman are absent from any meeting of the board, a chairman elected by the directors present from among themselves, shall preside at such meeting.

(6) No member of the Senate or the House of Assembly or a provincial council or the Legislative Assembly of the territory of South-West Africa may be appointed as a director and any director shall, on becoming such a member, vacate his office.

(7) Subject to the provisions of subsection (8), the corporation shall out of its funds pay to a director such remuneration and allowances, and afford him such transport facilities in respect of his services as a director, as the Minister in consultation with the Minister of Finance may determine.

(8) In respect of his sevices as a director any person in the full-time service of the State shall receive no remuneration and shall not be paid any allowances exceeding those payable to him in respect of his work in the service of the State.

(9) A director shall not be personally liable for any loss or damage arising out of or in connection with the execution of his duties, unless the loss or damage is due to anything done in bad faith or to gross negligence or to failure to comply with any provision of this Act.

5A. Committees.–(1) The corporation may establish committees to assist it in the performance of its functions and duties and appoint such persons, including members of the board or employees, as members of any such committee as it may deem fit.

(2) The members of a committee other than employees shall, out of the funds of the corporation, be paid such remuneration or allowances in respect of their services as may be determined by the Minister in consultation with the Minister of Finance.

[S. 5A inserted by s. 6 of Act No. 65 of 1972.]

5B. Delegation of powers.–(1) The corporation may delegate to any person or body of persons (including any member of the board, committee, employee, holder of a post with the corporation or a subsidiary company or any subsidiary company) any power conferred on the corporation by this Act.

(2) Where the corporation has delegated a power under subsection (1) to a person or body of persons referred to in that subsection, it may authorise such person or body to delegate the power in question to any other person or body of persons designated by the corporation.

(3) A delegation under subsections (1) and (2) may be made subject to such conditions or restrictions (if any) as may be determined by the corporation or by the person or body of persons making the delegation.

(4) The corporation shall not be divested of a power delegated by it or under its authority, and may amend or withdraw any decision made in the exercise of such power, including a decision amending or withdrawing a decision as contemplated in subsection (5).

(5) A person or body of persons referred to in subsection (1), shall not be divested of a power delegated by him or it, and may amend or withdraw any decision made in the exercise of such power.

(6) Where a power has been delegated to the holder of a post, such power shall be deemed to have been delegated to the person who at any time holds such post.

[S. 5B inserted by s. 6 of Act No. 65 of 1972.]

6. Share capital.–(1) The share capital of the corporation shall be one hundred million rand or such larger amount as the Minister may in consultation with the Minister of Finance from time to time on the recommendation of the board determine, and shall be divided into ordinary shares of one rand each.

(2) Shares in the corporation may be taken up by the State only and shall not be transferable.

(3) The State shall take up shares in the corporation to such extent and subject to such conditions as the Minister may in consultation with the Minister of Finance from time to time determine.

(4) Subject to the provisions of subsection (5), shares in the corporation shall be paid for out of moneys appropriated by Parliament for the purpose.

(5) Shares in the corporation, equal in value to the value of any undertakings or other financial interests of the Armaments Board taken over by the corporation in terms of this Act, shall be issued to the State free of charge, and no charge shall be made by the Armaments Board for the transfer of such undertakings or financial interests to the corporation.

(6) The value of the undertakings or financial interests referred to in subsection (5) shall be such value as the Minister may in consultation with the Minister of Finance determine.

6A. Loans.–(1) The corporation may, with the approval of the Minister granted in consultation with the Minister of Finance, raise money with or borrow or obtain money from any person or body at such rate of interest and on such conditions as the corporation may deem fit, issue debentures and, if necessary, provide security or make provision for the repayment of money so raised, borrowed or obtained.

(2) ......

[S. 6A inserted by s. 7 of Act No. 65 of 1972. Sub-s. (2) substituted by s. 6 of Act No. 20 of 1977 and repealed by s. 3 (1) of Act No. 21 of 1980.]

7. Limitation of liability of State.–The liability of the State as holder of the shares in the corporation shall be limited to the amount unpaid on shares held by it.

7A. Exemption from duties or fees.–The corporation or a subsidiary company shall be exempt from the payment of any duties or fees which, but for the provisions of this section, would in terms of a provision of any law (other than a law relating to customs and excise) have been payable to the State by the corporation or a subsidiary company in respect of any act or transaction or in respect of any document connected with any act or transaction.

[S. 7A inserted by s. 8 of Act No. 65 of 1972.]

7B. Funds of Corporation.–(1) The funds of the corporation shall consist of–

(*a*) the share capital mentioned in section 6;

(*b*) moneys appropriated by Parliament in order to enable the corporation to perform its functions;

    (*c*)   moneys raised, borrowed or obtained by the corporation in terms of section 6A (1);

    (*d*)   moneys obtained from any other source

(2) The corporation may receive donations or contributions from any person and shall use any moneys so acquired for such purposes and in accordance with such conditions as the donors or contributors may specify.

(3) The corporation may utilise any balance of its moneys remaining at the end of any financial year of the corporation for any expenses in connection with the performance of its functions.

[S. 7B inserted by s. 7 of Act No. 20 of 1977.]

8. Finances of corporation.–(1) The corporation shall, except in so far as this Act may otherwise provide, utilise all its assets solely for the attainment of its objects and matters incidental thereto, but may with the approval of the State President declare an annual dividend not exeeding eight per cent.

(1A) The corporation may establish a reserve fund for such purposes as, with due regard to subsection (1), it may deem fit and shall invest with the Public Debt Commissioners that portion of the moneys in the reserve fund which it does not required immediately.

[Sub-s. (1A) inserted by s. 9 (*a*) of Act No. 65 of 1972.]

(2) The board shall cause proper records to be kept of all the financial transactions, assets and liabilities of the corporation.

(3) The accounts of the corporation shall be audited annually by a person registered as an accountant and auditor under the provisions of the Public Accountants' and Auditors' Act, 1951 (Act No. 51 of 1951), and nominated annually by the Minister.

(4) As soon as may be after the completion of every audit the board shall furnish the Minister with the the report of the auditor containing such particulars as may be prescribed, together with a report on the activities of the corporation containing the prescribed particulars, and the Minister shall lay each report and any statements of account accompanying such report on the Table of Senate and of the House of Assembly within one month after receipt thereof by him, if Parliament is in ordinary session, or if Parliament is not in ordinary session, within one month after the commencement of the next ensuing

ordinary session, unless disclosure of any such report may in the opinion of the Minister jeopardise the safety of the State.

[Sub-s. (4) substituted by s. 9 (*b*) of Act No. 65 of 1972.]

(5) The board shall furnish the Minister with such information as he may call for from time to time in respect of the activities or financial position of the corporation.

8A. Employees' associations.–(1) (*a*) Any organisation of employees consisting solely of members of a prescribed category of employees may apply to the corporation for recognition as an employees' association.

(*b*) An application referred to in subsection (1) (*a*) shall be made in writing and in the prescribed form and manner and shall be accompanied by three copies of the constitution of the organisation of employees so applying (duly certified as true copies under the signature of the chairman and the secretary of that organisation) and such other documents or information as may be prescribed.

(*c*) An organisation of employees applying for recognition under this section, shall furnish the corporation with such further information as the corporation may require, within the period fixed by the corporation.

(2) The corporation may, before it grants the said application, require the organisation of employees so applying for recognition to give notice thereof to such employees' associations or organisations of employees as the corporation may specifiy.

(3) (*a*) An employees' association or an organisation of employees which has applied for recognition as an employees' association and whose application is still pending or an organisation of employees which intends so to apply, may, subject to the provisions of paragraph (*b*) and within a period of thirty days from the date of the notification referred to in subsection (2), in writing lodge with the corporation an objection to an application referred to in subsection (1).

(*b*) An objection referred to in paragraph (*a*) shall specify the grounds thereof and a copy thereof shall at the same time be delivered to the organisation of employees whose application is being objected to.

(c) An employees' association or organisation of employees so objecting, shall furnish the corporation with such further information as the corporation may require, within the period fixed by the corporation.

(4) (a) No organisation of employees which applies to the corporation for recognition as an employees' association shall be recognised as an employees' association by the corporation unless the corporation is satisfied that–

> (i) the consitution of that organisation complies with the provisions of this Act;

> (ii) the interests of the employees concerned will be promoted by such an employees' association, if recognised; and

> (iii) that organisation has not been established in order to harm the interests of other employees or is not likely to harm the said interests.

(b) The corporation may refuse to recognise an organisation of employees as an employees' association if it is of the opinion that the interests of the employees concerned are already adequately promoted and served by an existing employees' association or if the organisation in question fails to amend any provision of its constitution in a manner indicated by the corporation in writing or to delete from such constitution any such provision so indicated by the corporation or to insert in such constitution any provision so indicated by the corporation.

(c) The corporation shall not recognise an organisation of employees as an employees' association if the membership of the proposed employees' association would be open to both white and non-white employees.

(d) When the corporation recognises an organisation of employees as an employees' association, it shall issue a certificate of recognition to that employees' association.

(e) The corporation may in writing withdraw a certificate issued under paragraph (d) if it is of the opinion that the grounds upon which the recognition has been granted no longer exist or if the employees' associated in question fails to comply with any of the provisions of section 8B (3).

(5) When an application in terms of subsection (1) for recognition as an employees' association is refused by the corporation or when the corporation in terms of subsection (4) (*e*) withdraws a certificate of recognition, the organisation of employees in question may in the prescribed manner appeal to the Minister against that refusal or withdrawal and the Minister may, after consideration of such an appeal–

(*a*) confirm the said refusal or withdrawal by the corporation;

(*b*) direct the corporation to grant the said application or to cancel the said withdrawal, as the case may be; or

(*c*) direct the corporation, on compliance by the appellant with conditions stipulated by the Minister, to grant the said application or to cancel the said withdrawal, as the case may be.

[S. 8A inserted by s. 10 of Act No. 65 of 1972.]

8B. Constitution of employees' association.–(1) The constitution of every employees' association shall contain provisions not inconsistent with this Act in regard to the following matters:

(*a*) the objects of the association;

(*b*) the category and race of employees to whom membership of the association shall be open;

(*c*) the qualifications for membership and the membership fees and other moneys (if any) to be paid by members or the method of determining such fees;

(*d*) the circumstances and the manner in which the membership of a member may be terminated;

(*e*) the manner in which a member may terminate his membership;

(*f*) the benefits to which members are or may become entitled;

(*g*) the circumstances in which a member shall cease to be entitled to the benefits of membership;

(*h*) the acquisition and control of property;

(*i*) the purposes for which its funds may be used;

(*j*) the calling and conduct of meetings of members and the keeping of minutes of the proceedings at such meetings;

(*k*) the establishment of and the powers, duties and functions of a management committee and other committees (if any);

(*l*) the procurement to be followed in the appointment or election of members of the management committee or any other committee;

(*m*) the body or bodies to which a member shall have the right to appeal against a decision given on any matter referred to in paragraph (*d*) or (*g*) by the management committee or any other committee having the power to give such a decision in terms of the constitution and the manner in which such appeal shall be prosecuted and determined;

(*n*) the circumstances and the manner in which any member of the management committee or of any other committee may be removed from office: Provided that, in addition to any other provision made in terms of this paragraph, provision shall be made for the taking of a ballot, at the written request of a specified number or proportion of the members, to determine whether a member of the management committee or any other committee, named in the request, shall be removed from office or, if so removed, shall be reinstated;

(*o*) the alteration of the constitution;

(*p*) the dissolution of the association; and

(*q*) any other matter which the corporation may determine.

(2) (*a*) An employees' association may alter its constitution in the manner determined in its constitution.

(*b*) Three copies of a resolution to alter the constitution of an employees' association shall be transmitted to the corporation by the secretary of that association and the said alteration shall only be of force and effect if the corporation issues a certificate of approval to that alteration to the employees' association in question.

(3) Every employees' association shall–

(*a*) maintain a register of members showing their names, the membership fees (if any) paid by each member and the periods to which those payments relate;

(*b*) keep proper books of account;

(*c*) annually within a period of six months from the date of expiry of its last preceding financial year–

(i) prepare a statement of income and expenditure during that financial year and a balance sheet showing its financial position at the expiry of that financial year;

(ii) cause its books of account to be audited by a public accountant; and

(iii) furnish the corporation with a copy of its audited balance sheet.

[S. 8B inserted by s. 10 of Act No. 65 of 1972.]

8C. Disputes between employees and employers.–(1) (*a*) An individual employee may within the prescribd period and in the prescribed manner personally make written representations to his employer with regard to a matter relating exclusively to that employee and which is connected with his circumstances of employment or the conditions of employment which apply to him or with regard to the termination of his employment by his employer.

(*b*) The employer shall in writing notify the employee of his decision with regard to the representations.

(*c*) If the employee is not satisfied with his employer's decision as notified in terms of paragraph (*b*), the employee may within the prescribed period and in the prescribed manner refer the matter to the advisory committee referred to in subsection (3) (*a*), which, after it has investigated the matter, shall submit to the corporation such recommendations about it as it may deem fit.

(*d*) The corporation may accept, reject or amend the said recommendations or make such other decision with regard to the matter in question as it may deem fit, and shall in writing notify the employee of its decision in that regard.

(*e*) If the employee is not satisfied with the corporation's decision as notified in terms of paragraph (*d*), the employee may, within the prescribed period and in the prescribed manner, give notice to the Minister accordingly and it shall thereupon be deemed, for the purposes of section 8D, that a dispute exists between the employee and his employer with regard to the matter or termination of employment in question.

(2) (*a*) An employees' association may, within the prescribed period and in the prescribed manner, on behalf of two or more employees who are members thereof, make written representations to their employer with regard to the employment of other employees by the employer or with regard to a matter which is connected with their circumstances of employment or the conditions of employment which apply to them.

(*b*) The employer shall in writing notify the employees' association of his decision with regard to the representations.

(*c*) If the employees concerned are not satisfied with their employer's decision as notified in terms of paragraph (*b*), the employees' association shall, at the request of those employees, within the prescribed period and in the prescribed manner refer the matter to the advisory committee referred to in subsection (3) (*b*), which, after it has investigated the matter, shall submit to the corporation such recommendations about it as it may deem fit.

(*d*) The corporation may accept, reject or amend the said recommendation or make such other decision with regard to the matter in question as it may deem fit, and shall in writing notify the employees' association of its decision in that regard.

(*e*) If the employees concerned are not satisfied with the corporation's decision as notified in terms of paragraph (*d*), the employees' association shall, if so requested by the said employees, within the prescribed period and in the prescribed manner, give notice to the Minister accordingly and it shall thereupon be deemed, for the purposes of section 8D, that a dispute exists between the employees concerned and their employer with regard to the employment or matter in question.

(3) An advisory committee shall consist of–

(*a*) in the case of an advisory committee referred to in subsection (1) (*c*), two or more persons designated by the corporation (one of whom shall be designated by the corporation as chairman of the advisory committee so referred to), and, if the employee concerned wishes to do so, and equal number of persons as the number of persons designated by the corporation in terms of this paragraph, designated by the employee concerned within the prescribed period, from among members of the management committee of the employees' association of which he is a member: Provided that if the said employee fails so to designate persons, the said advisory committee shall consist only of the persons designated by the corporation in terms of this paragraph;

(b) in the case of an advisory committee referred to in subsection (2) (c)–

   (i) two persons designated by the corporation, one of whom shall be designated by the corporation as chairman of the advisory committee so referred to;

   (ii) if a subsidiary company is the employer referred to in subsection (2) (a), a member of the directorate of that subsidiary company, to be designated by the subsidiary company; and

   (iii) an equal number of persons as the number of persons designated in terms of subparagraph (i) or subparagraphs (i) and (ii), as the case may be, to be designated by the employees' association which has made the representations as contemplated in subsection (2) (a), from among members of the management committee of the said employees' association.

(4) The advisory committee referred to in subsection (3) (a) or (3) (b), as the case may be, shall perform its functions in the prescribed manner.

[S. 8C inserted by s. 10 of Act No. 65 of 1972.]

8D. Settlement Board.–(1) When a dispute is in terms of section 8C (1) (e) or 8C (2) (e) deemed to exist, the Minister shall, subject to the provisions of subsection (2), appoint three persons as members of a board, in this Act referred to as the Settlement Board, to settle the said dispute in terms of the provisions of this Act.

(2) The Minister shall appoint as members of the Settlement Board–

(a)   one person to be designated as chairman by the Minister and who shall be a judge of the Supreme Court of South Africa or a magistrate of the rank known as principal magistrate or an equivalent or higher rank or an advocate of not less than ten years standing or a person who was such a judge or magistrate;

(b)   one person from among at least three and not more than five persons whose names have been submitted for that purpose by the corporation; and

(c)   one person from among at least three and not more than five persons whose names have been submitted for that purpose, in the case of a dispute contemplated in section 8C (1) (e), by the employee concerned, or, in the case of a dispute contemplated in section 8C (2) (e), by the employees' association in question.

(3) If the office of any member of the Settlement Board appointed under subsection (1) becomes vacant at any time before the settlement of a dispute for the settlement of which such Settlement Board has been appointed, the Minister shall, subject to the provisions of subsection (2), appoint another person to hold office and the proceedings for the settlement of the dispute in question shall be proceeded with as if the member so substituted had been a member of the Settlement Board from the commencement of the said proceedings.

(4) There shall be paid to a member of the Settlement Board (other than a member in the full-time service of the State, the corporation or a subsidiary company) in respect of his service as such, such remuneration and allowances out of the funds of the corporation as the Minster in consultation with the Minister of Finance may from time to time determine.

[S. 8D inserted by s. 10 of Act No. 65 of 1972.]

8E.   Submission of documents.–(1) The Minister shall, as soon as practicable after he has appointed the Settlement Board referred to in section 8D, in the prescribed manner give notice thereof to the employee or employees' association concerned, as the case may be.

(2) The said employee or employees' association, as the case may be, shall submit to the Settlement Board a copy of, as the case may be–

(a) the representations referred to in section 8C (1) (a) or 8C (2) (a);

(b) the employer's notification referred to in section 8C (1) (b) or 8C (2) (b); and

(c) the corporation's notification referred to in section 8C (1) (d) or 8C (2) (d),

within the prescribed period after the date of the notification referred to in subsection (1).

[S. 8E inserted by s. 10 of Act No. 65 of 1972.]

8F. Decisions of the Settlement Board.–(1) The decision of the majority of the members of the Settlement Board shall be deemed to be the decision of that Board.

(2) The decision of the Settlement Board in respect of a dispute shall be final and shall bind the parties to the dispute and the corporation, but, except in the case of a dispute with regard to the termination of the employment of an employee by his employer, only for such period as the Settlement Board may determine.

[S. 8F inserted by s. 10 of Act No. 65 of 1972.]

8G. Prohibition of strikes.–(1) No employee or other person shall instigate a strike or incite any employee to take part in or continue a strike, and no employee shall take part in a strike or in the continuation of a strike.

(2) (a) When an employee employed in a particular department, branch or division of the corporation or a subsidiary company is charged with having taken part in a strike or in the continuation of a strike in contravention of the provisions of subsection (1) and it is proved that concerted action as defined in paragraph (b) took place in that department, branch or division during the period covered by the charge and that the accused was at any time during that period engaged upon work or a type of work with respect to the performance of which such a departure from standards, methods, procedures or practices as referred to in subparagraph (i) of that paragraph had occurred–

(i) such concerted action shall be deemed to constitute a retardation of the progress of work or an obstruction of work as contemplated in the definition of "strike" in section 1;

(ii) the accused shall be deemed to have taken part in such concerted action unless he proves that he was opposed to that action and in fact took no part in it and that during the period covered by the charge he openly dissociated himself from that action.

(b) The concerted action referred to in paragraph (a) is any concerted action on the part of any number of employees which—

(i) involves a departure from standards, methods, procedures or practices which had previously been maintained, adopted or observed by those employees as their normal and regular routine in or in connection with the performance of their work;

(ii) has resulted in a diminution in the output or a reduction in the rate of work or a prolongation of the time normally taken to perform particular tasks in the department, branch or division in question of the corporation or a subsidiary company; and

(iii) by reason of any of the circumstances referred to in subparagraph (ii) has had, or was likely to have if continued, a detrimental effect upon the normal production of the corporation or a subsidiary company or upon the efficiency, in general, of the corporation or a subsidiary company.

(3) When an employee or other person is charged under this section with having instigated a strike or with having incited an employee to take part in or to continue a strike, or when an employee is so charged with having taken part in a strike or in the continuation of a strike and a refusal, failure, retardation, obstruction, breach or termination as contemplated in the definition of "strike" in section 1 (as amplified by subsection (2) of this section), and stated in the charge, is proved, it shall be presumed until the contrary is proved, that the refusal, failure, retardation, obstruction, breach or termination was in pursuance of such a collusion, agreement or understanding and for such a purpose as contemplated in the said definition and stated in the charge.

(4) An employee or other person who contravenes the provisions of subsection (1) shall be guilty of an offence and liable on

conviction to a fine not exceeding one thousand rand or to imprisonment for a period not exceeding five years or to such imprisonment without the option of a fine or to both such fine and such imprisonment.

[S. 8G inserted by s. 10 of Act No. 65 of 1972.]

9. Regulations.–The State President may make regulations in regard to–

(a) the place where the head office of the corporation shall be situated;

(b) conditions or restrictions subject to which the board shall manage and control the affairs of the corporation, including the circumstances in which the board shall manage and control such affairs subject to the approval of the State President or the Minister or the Minister acting in consultation with any other Minister of State and the manner in which such affairs shall be managed and controlled in particular circumstances or in relation to companies promoted by the corporation;

[Para. (b) substituted by s. 11 (a) of Act No. 65 of 1972.]

(c) the calling of and procedure and quorum at meetings of the board, including the manner of voting and the number of votes required for a decision of the board;

(d) the preservation of secrecy in regard to the affairs of the corporation;

(e) the keeping of records, minutes and books of account;

(f) the contents of auditors' or other reports to be furnished to the Minister by the board;

(g) the date on which the financial year of the corporation shall terminate;

(h) the manner of calculating the price at which and the circumstances in which armaments shall be supplied by the corporation to the State, whether in general or in particular cases;

(hA) any matter which in terms of this Act shall or may be prescribed by way of regulation;

[Para. (hA) inserted by s. 11 (b) of Act No. 65 of 1972.]

(*i*)   generally, all matters for which he deems it necessary or expedient to make regulations in order to achieve the objects of this Act.

10.   Winding up of corporation.–The corporation shall not be wound up except by or under the authority of an Act of Parliament.

11.   Use of name of corporation.–No person shall carry on business and no company shall be registered under the Companies Act, 1926 (Act No. 46 of 1926), under or by a name in which the expression "Armscor" or "Krygkor" appears or which is identical with the name of the corporation or which so nearly resembles such name as to be calculated to deceive: Provided that this section shall not prohibit any person from carrying on business or remaining registered under or by a name under or by which such person carried on business or was registered at the commencement of this Act.

11A.   Prohibition of disclosure of certain information.–(1) No person shall disclose to any person any information in relation to the acquisition, supply, marketing, importation, export, development, manufacture, maintenance or repair of or research in connection with armaments by, for, on behalf of or for the benefit of the corporation or a subsidiary company, except on the written authority of the Minister or of a person authorised thereto by the Minister.

(2) The provisions of subsection (1) shall not prohibit the disclosure of information–

(*a*)   by any person in so far as it is necessary for the performance of his functions in connection with the acquisition, supply, marketing, importation, export, development, manufacture, maintenance or repair of or research in connection with armaments by, for, on behalf of or for the benefit of the corporation or a subsidiary company;

(*b*)   released for publication by the Minister or by a person authorised thereto by the Minister.

(3) Any person who contravenes the provisions of subsection (1), shall be guilty of an offence and liable on conviction to a fine not exceeding fifteen thousand rand or to imprisonment for a period not exceeding eight years or to both such fine and such imprisonment.

[S. 11A inserted by s. 4 of Act No. 86 of 1980.]

12. Exemption of corporation from provisions of certain laws.– (1) Subject to the provisions of subsection (2), the provisions of the Companies Act, 1926 (Act No. 46 of 1926), or of any other law relating to companies, shall not apply with reference to the corporation.

(2) The State President may by proclamation in the *Gazette* apply to the corporation any provision of the said Act or other law, not inconsistent with the provisions of this Act, with such modifications as may be specified in the proclamation.

(3) The State President may by like proclamation exempt the corporation or a subsidiary company from the provisions of such laws as may be specified in the proclamation, to the extent so specified.

[Sub-s. (3) substituted by s. 12 of Act No. 65 of 1972.]

(4) The State President may from time to time in like manner repeal or amend any proclamation issued under this section.

12A. Act 28 of 1956 not applicable.–(1) Subject to the provisions of subsection (2) the provisions of the Industrial Conciliation Act, 1956 (Act No. 28 of 1956), or any amendment thereof, shall not apply to the corporation, or a subsidiary company as employer, or to an employee of the corporation or a subsidiary company in respect of his employment as such.

(2) The State President may by proclamation in the *Gazette* apply to the corporation or a subsidiary company as employer or to an employee of the corporation or a subsidiary company in respect of his employment as such, any provision of the said Act, not inconsistent with the provisions of this Act, with such modifications as may be specified in the proclamation.

[S. 12A inserted by s. 13 of Act No. 65 of 1972.]

13. Repeal of Act 87 of 1964.–(1) Subject to the provisions of section 2A (1) (*b*) and subsection (2) of this section, the Armaments Act, 1964, is hereby repealed.

(2) Subject to the provisions of section 2A (1) (*b*), anything done under any provision of the Armaments Act, 1964, which could have been done under any provision of the Act, shall be deemed to have been done under such latter provision.

[S. 13 inserted by s. 8 of Act No. 20 of 1977.]

14. Short title.–This Act shall be called the Armaments Development and Production Act, 1968.

Appendix D

Highlights of Armscor's Accomplishments

–The Cheetah, South Africa's Supersonic Fighter Aircraft is an Upgraded Version of the Mirage III.
–The Ratel infantry combat vehicle is regarded as one of the best in the world.
–The logistical Ratel was designed as a support vehicle for troops operating away from their base.
–The 155 mm G5-Howitzer gun is regarded by weapons experts worldwide as the most effective in its class.
–The G5 has a range of almost 40 km.
–The G6, a motorised, highly mobile version of the G5, is described as one of the most sophisticated weapons ever produced by Armscor.
–A flotilla of strike vessels of the Minister's class was designed and built for the South African Navy. Designed in accordance with the international move to smaller, more manoeuvrable ships, these vessels possess an exceptional strike capability for their size.
–One of the Air Force's most devastating weapons is the highly sophisticated Kukri missile, designed for air combat. Built in South Africa, the Kukri is operated with an advanced helmet-sighting system developed locally. A fighter pilot sees the 'enemy' through the sighting system built into his helmet.
–Over the years, a range of mortars has been produced for the Defence Force.
–Weapons designed to function with maximum efficiency under bush war conditions are developed by Armscor on an ongoing basis. Rifles and shotguns produced by Musgrave in Bloemfontein are

manufactured with infinite care by skilled craftsmen and are sought worldwide.

–The 5.56 millimetre R4 assault rifle is acclaimed by both arms exports and soldiers in the field as an excellent addition to the heavier R1.

–Armscor produces about 150 types of ammunition, from calibres for small handguns to the largest aircraft bombs required by the Defence Force.

–Among the greatest advances made during the last few years, have been those in the area of sophisticated communication systems.

–Eloptro, one of Armscor's subsidiaries, develops the electro-optical equipment required for the manufacture of the country's advanced weapon systems.

–Compact data entry terminals make it possible for troops in the operational area to feed information directly into a central computer for processing.

–Ingenious breakthroughs in areas such as frequency-hopping has created confidential communication channels between combat troops and their bases.

–Equipment developed by Armscor creates a communications umbrella covering a whole operational area.

–Extensive research, covering a wide range of areas, forms the basis of Armscor's on-going development and improvement of weapons systems.

–To provide for the needs of a modern defence force, Armscor established a self-contained industry for the development and production of armaments after the compulsory arms embargo imposed by the United Nations in 1977. The industry not only includes all manufacturing processes, but also on-going research and quality control.

–The 120 kilogramme shrapnel bomb was developed for ground attack by supersonic fighter aircraft. Prefragmentation is achieved by a layer of steel balls cast in epoxy between the outer fibreglass skin and the explosive core.

–A servo-controlled machine gun configuration is ideally suited for use in helicopters and infantry combat vehicles.

–The development of a locally designed gas turbine engine was another major breakthrough for Armscor. The engine is characterised by low cost simplicity of design, reliability and minimal maintenance.

–The SA Navy's replenishment ship *SAS Drakensberg* is at 12,500 tons, the largest vessel to be designed and built locally.

–The latest addition to South Africa's air defences is known as the XTP1. This locally designed helicopter is based on the well-known Puma and is equipped with an impressive array of weapons.

–The announcement in 1986 of an experimental tandem combat helicopter represented an important breakthrough in the aeronautical field.

–The development of air supply platforms enables the SADF to deliver supplies and equipment to combat troops in remote areas or behind enemy lines.

–Armscor has developed an extensive range of military vehicles in conjunction with the private sector. These vehicles, collectively known as the SAMIL range, are considered by overseas experts to be among the toughest and most reliable available.

–A range of mine-resistant vehicles, based on a concept evolved in South Africa, has also been developed. These vehicles can detonate any conventional landmine without injury to the occupants.

–Weaponry such as the SS-77 machine gun is in concept and manufacture wholly South African. As in the case of all weapons systems developed by Armscor, the SS-77 has been tested extensively under battle conditions.

–The large tracts of land under Armscor's control are managed in close collaboration with the various departments of nature conservation.

–The Erasmus Castle is one of the architectural landmarks of Pretoria. It is being fully restored as part of the development of Armscor's new head office complex.

–Great care has been taken to ensure the best possible working environment for Armscor's 23,00 staff members.

–On 22 October 1988, Armscor introduced the Rooikat meaning "red cat" (Lynx) in Afrikaans. This fast and highly manoeuvrable vehicle is designed to "seek and destroy deep in enemy territory." It has a 76 mm gun and an operating range of 620 miles at speeds of 75 mph on paved roads. The Rooikat can travel cross country at 37 mph, its eight-wheel drive powering it up gradients to 70 percent. Its rapid firing 76 mm computer-assisted gun can hit tanks at a range of 1.25 miles.

–Test launching of a new nuclear capability intermediate-range ballistic missile is scheduled for the latter part of 1989.

Source: Armscor, 'A giant in South African Industry', undated, pp. 1–20.

Chapter Notes

Chapter 1

1. *The Military Balance 1988/89*, published by the International Institute for the Strategic Studies, London, and *Defence*, 'South African Defence Budget up by Almost 30%', August 1987, p. 450.
2. *South African Digest*, 'Almost Self-Sufficient', 13 September 1985, p. 833.
3. *South African Digest*, 'New Milestones for SAAF', 18 July 1986, p. 639
4. Ibid., p. 639.
5. 'A U.S. Policy Toward South Africa', Department of State, *The Report of the Secretary of State's Advisory Committee on South Africa*, 29 January 1987, p. 21.
6. Ibid., p. 29.
7. UN Security Council Resolution, 418, of 4 November 1977.
8. *This is Armscor*, prepared and printed by Armscor, undated, p. 2.
9. Ibid., p. 2.
10. Interview with 'Commandant Piet Marais, Chairman of South Africa's Armscor', *International Defence Review*, Vol. 17, No. 10, 1984, p. 1565.
11. 'The New Role of South Africa's Security Establishment', *Munger Africana Library Notes*, K.W. Grundy, March 1985, p.11, quoted from C. Wright Mills, *The Power Elite* (New York: Oxford University Press, 1956), esp. chaps. 9 and 12. 'The Business of Defence', *Financial Mail*, Vol. 62, No. 9 (26 November 1976), pp. 797–98; 'Armscor: Behind the Secrecy Shroud', *Financial Mail*, Vol. 81, No. 11 (11 September 1981), pp. 1240–41; *Sunday Times*, 11 July 1982, p. 25; RSA, DOD, *White Paper on Defence, 1984*, pp. 19–20; 'Krygkor/Armscor', Supplement to *Paratus*, Vol. 33, No. 11 (November 1982); *The Star*, WAE, 5 September 1983, p. 8; and 'Armscor Curb Costs', *Financial Mail*, Vol. 90, No. 10 (9 December 1993), p. 74.
12. Grundy, p. 12.
13. See *International Defence Review*, Vol. 16, No. 3, 1983; *South African Defence Force*, January 1985; *Armada International*, March/April 1983.

Chapter 2

1. *New York Times*, 6 December 1963, p. 6, C. 8.
2. *New York Times*, 12 February 1963, p. 1, C. 7.
3. *New York Times*, 9 July 1963, p. 6, C. 7.
4. *New York Times*, 3 August 1963, p. 1, C. 5.
5. *New York Times*, 4 August 1963, p. 23, C. 1.

6. *New York Times*, 7 August 1963, p. 3, C. 1.
7. *New York Times*, 7 August 1963, p. 3, C. 1.
8. *New York Times*, 14 August 1963, p. 7, C. 4.
9. *New York Times*, 19 September 1963, p. 1, C. 4.
10. *New York Times*, 10 October 1963, p. 8, C. 3.
11. *Committee of Foreign Affairs – House of Representatives – Hearings, 89th Congress*, 2nd Session, 1 March 1966.
12. *The Unnatural Alliance*, James Adams, p. 86, cited in *The Link*, 'The Israeli-South African-Israeli Alliance', Jane Hunter, p. 7.
13. Hunter, p. 7.
14. *Foreign Policy*, 'South Africa: Straight Talk on Sanctions', William Minter, No. 65, Winter 86–87, p. 58.
15. Minter, p. 58.
16. *Hearings*, House, 89th Congress, 1 March 1966.
17. Minter, p. 58.
18. *Hearings*, House, 89th Congress, 1 March 1966.
19. *Hearings*, House, 89th Congress, 2 March 1966, p. 53.
20. *Hearings*, House, 89th Congress, 2 March 1966, p. 61.
21. *South Africa's Defence Strategy*, Abdul S. Minty, UN, Centre Against Apartheid, Department of Political and Security Affairs, January 1976, p. 3.
22. Minter, p. 8 and *South African Digest*, March 1973, p. 16, *The Sunday Times*, Johannesburg, October 1973, p. 21.
23. *The Apartheid War Machine*, International Defence and Aid Fund, April 1980, p. 12.
24. Ibid., p. 14 cited sources, *SA Digest*, 6 December 1974, these organisations, though established in 1964, were instituted in law by the Armaments Development and Production Act, No. 57 of 1968, *House of Assembly Debates*, Cape Town, 9 September 1974, The South African system differs from the French to a certain extent in the level of nationalisation of the industry.
25. Ibid., p. 14, cited from *Financial Gazette*, 15 July 1977, Statement by Armscor's Chairman Commandant Piet Marais.
26. Ibid., p. 15.
27. Ibid., p. 17.
28. Ibid., p. 17, also *South African Foundation Information Digest, 1987,* indicates that the defence budget has increased every year since 1973. As of the 1986/87 financial year funds voted were 5.12 billion rand, 13.7% of state expenditure and 3.5% of GNP.
29. *The Citizen*, Johannesburg, 23 September 1986.
30. *Beeld*, Johannesburg, 23 September 1986.
31. *Forbes*, 'Economic Sanctions Aren't Working', 9 March 1987, p. 102.
32. *Forbes*, p. 104.
33. *U.S. Arms Transfers to South Africa in Violation of the United Nations Voluntary Arms Embargo: 1963–1977*, Sean Gervasi, UN, Centre Against Apartheid, September 1978, p. 1.
34. Gervasi, p. 3.
35. Gervasi, p. 12.
36. *Rand Daily Mail*, 27 April, 1972.
37. *Sunday Star*, Johannesburg, 9 February 1986.
38. Ibid.
39. *Los Angeles Times*, 'Israel to End Arms Sales to S. Africa,' Dan Fisher, March 1987.
40. *Committee on Foreign Affairs – House of Representatives – Hearings, 99th Congress*, 1st Session, 17 April 1985, p. 88.

41. *Hearings*, House, 99th Congress, 17 April 1985, p. 106.
42. *Hearings*, House, 99th Congress, 17 April 1985, p. 106.
43. *International Defense Review*, 'South Africa Starts Arms Export Drive', Robert Boyle, 1983, p. 268.
44. *International Defense Review*, 1983, p. 268.
45. *Hearings*, House, 99th Congress, 17 April 1985, p. 133.
46. *Bulletin of the Atomic Scientists*, 'South Africa Circumvents Embargo', quoted from *The 1985 South African Computer User's Handbook* (Johannesburg: Systems and Publishers, 1985), pp. Q38, 62, 112. 'Naschem at Pemex '83', *Machine Tool and Product Engineering Journal*, July 1983. Reed Kramer, 'Proposed Aircraft Sales to S. Africa Tests New Trade Policy.' *Washington Post*, 16 March 1982, p. A20.
47. *Bulletin*, p. 10, also *Africa News*, 'Israel and Taiwan Embrace Homelands', 27 November 1983, pp. 6–8.
48. *Datamation*, 'S. Africa; Pulling the Plug', Willie Schatz, 1 October 1985, p. 4.
49. *Bulletin*, p. 111, quoted from an unpublished quarterly and annual reports compiled by the Department of Defence pursuant to Section 36 of the Arms Export Control Act (various issues): disclosures to the American Friends Service Committee under the Freedom of Information Act by the Office of the Legal Advisor to the State Department's Bureau of Politico-Military Affairs by telephone on 27 October 1983 and on 10 November 1983, and by correspondence dated 28 November, 1983.
50. *Bulletin*, p. 12.
51. *Declaration of the International Seminar on the UN Arms Embargo Against South Africa*, London, 28–30 May 1986, UN A/41/388, S/1812, 2 June 1986, p. 5.
52. *Declaration of the World Conference on Sanctions Against Racist South Africa*, Paris, 16–20 June 1986, from UN Transmittal Sheet A/41/434. S/18185, dtd. 30 June 1986, pp. 10–11.
53. *International Seminar*, p. 7.
54. *International Seminar*, p. 7.
55. *White Paper on Defence and Armaments Supply*, RSA, Department of Defence, 1986, p. 33.
56. *White Paper*, 1986, p. iii.
57. *Washington Post*, 'US Allies Selling Arms to S. Africa', 28 March 1987, p. A1.

Chapter 3
1. *This is Armscor*, prepared and printed by Armscor, undated, p. 2.
2. Ibid., p. 2.
3. *Washington Times*, 'Sanctions Called Aid to Forces of Revolution', 26 March 1987, p. 6A., c. 6.
4. *Bulletin of the Atomic Scientists*, 'South Africa Circumvents Embargo', Thomas Conrad, March 1986, p. 8.
5. *Navy International*, 'The South African Navy', Helmoed-Römer Heitman, March 1986, p. 82.
6. *Navy International*, March 1986, p. 82.
7. *Defense and Foreign Affairs Handbook*, 1986, p. 662.
8. *South African Digest*, 'New Impetus for the Navy', 9 May 1986, pp. 400–401.
9. *South African Digest*, 'Base Praised', 13 September 1985, p. 833, cited in the foreword of *Jane's Fighting Ships*, 1985, 1986.
10. *South African Digest*, 'Navy Shows Its Punch', 20 March 1987, p. 17; *Beeld* and *South African Press Association*, 16 March 1987.
11. *South African Digest*, 'A Show of Force', 21 March 1986, p. 245.
12. Ibid., p. 245.

13. *South African Broadcasting Company*, 'Beating the Arms Boycott', 11 March 1986.
14. *SABC*, 11 March 1986.
15. *South African Digest*, 'SA's New Helicopter', 14 March 1986, p. 216.
16. *South African Digest*, 'SA Air Force More Self-Sufficient', 18 July 1986, p. 640.
17. *Eastern Province Herald*, 17 July 1986.
18. *Beeld*, Johannesburg, 'Cheeta', 17 July 1986.
19. *Financial Mail*, 'Armscor's Big Push', 9 November 1984.
20. *Armed Forces*, 'The Ingwe', July 1986, Vol. 5, p. 15.
21. *The Unnatural Alliance*, John Adams, 1984, p. 86.
22. *Morning Edition, National Public Radio*, 'Israel and South Africa: A lively Arms Trade', 13 January 1986.
23. *Washington Times*, 'U.S. Charges Allies Violate Arms Embargo', 2 April 1987, p. A1, c. 5.
24. *Washington Times*, 'Sanctions Law Squeezes Some Friends of Israel', 2 April 1987, p. A4, c. 2.
25. Ibid., p. A4, c. 2.
26. *Washington Times*, 'Report Call Israel's Worst Pact Violators', 3 April 1987, p. 3A, c. 1.
27. *Washington Post*, 'State Dept. Lists Allies Arming S. Africa', 3 April 1987, A34, c. 1.
28. See *Armada International*, Mar./Apr. 1983, *This is Armscor*, no date, *Armscor*, circa 1987 and *Business Day*, 3 July 1987.
29. 'The Corporate Power Elite in South Africa: Interlocking Directorships Among Large Enterprises', *Political Geography Quarterly*, B.A. Cox and C.M. Rogerson, Vol. 4. No. 3, July 1985, p. 223.
30. Cox and Rogerson, p. 223.
31. Cox and Rogerson, p. 228.
32. Grundy, p. 14.
33. Grundy, p. 20.

Chapter 4

1. 'The Industrialisation Challenge', *South Africa International*, Johan C. Van Zyl, Vol. 17, No. 2, October 1986, p. 71.
2. Johan C. Van Zyl, p. 71.
3. Johan C. Van Zyl, p. 72.
4. *Washington Times*, 'Debt-Wracked Zimbabwe Buys Top-of-Line Soviet Jets', Peter Almond, 13 April 1987 and 'Soviet Sale of 12 Jets to Zimbabwe Confirmed', *Combined Dispatches*, 14 April 1987.
5. *Jane's All the World's Aircraft*, 1985–86.
6. *International Defense Review*, Vol. 17, No. 10, 1984, p. 1567.
7. *Survey of Race Relations in South Africa* 1983, Carole Cooper, *et al.* Research Staff, South African Institute of Race Relations, Johannesburg, 1984, p. 582.
8. *The Citizen*, 'SADF Computerises Stock', 26 February 1987.
9. Quoted in *South African Digest*, 27 March 1987.
10. *The Economist*, 'The Israeli Connection', 5 November 1977, p. 90.
11. *U.S. News and World Report*, 'Analysis: Why Afrikaners Believe They Can Hold On For Years; Is South Africa Invulnerable?', 23 March 1987.
12. Reuters Ltd., 31 March 1987, International News, 'SOUTH AFRICAN ARMS EXPERT SAYS ISRAEL NOT ESSENTIAL, JOHANNESBURG, S. AFRICA – ISRAEL', LEAD: The head of South Africa's state-owned armaments maker has said his country is not dependent on Israel, which recently said it would not sign new defence contracts with Pretoria.

13. Reuters Ltd., 1 April 1987, International News, 'SOUTH AFRICA BOASTS SUCCESS IN DEFEATING ARMS EMBARGO', JOHANNESBURG, S AFRICA-ARMS, LEAD: South Africa, target of a decade-old UN arms embargo, said today its weapons industry was so advanced it was now the third largest foreign currency earner after mining and agriculture.
14. The British Broadcasting Corporation; Summary of World Broadcasts, 2 April 1987, Part 4, The Middle East, Africa and Latin America; B. AFRICA ME/8532/B/1, Commentary Stresses South Africa's Independence in Weapons, Johannesburg home service in English.
15. *The British Broadcasting Corporation*; Summary of World Broadcasts, 15 March 1986, Saturday, Part 4 The Middle East, Africa and Latin America; B. AFRICA, ME/8208/b/1, Growth of Armaments Industry in South Africa, Johannesburg home service in English.
16. *The British Broadcasting Corporation*; Summary of World Broadcasts, 18 July 1986, Friday, Part 4 The Middle East, Africa and Latin America; B. AFRICA, ME/8314/b/1, S African Comment on 'Spectacular Failure' of Weapons Sanctions, Johannesburg home service in English.
17. *Business Week*, 'How the World Keeps The Iran-Iraq War Going', 29 December 1986, p. 46.
18. *Business Week*, p. 47.
19. *Business Week*, p. 47.
20. *Armada International*, 'The Advances Made in Air-to-Ground Weapon Systems', April 1987, p. 52.

Chapter 5
1. Statutes of the Republic of South Africa – Defence, *Defence Special Account Act, No. 6 of 1974.*
2. *Pretoria's Praetorians*, Philip H. Frankel, Cambridge University Press, London, 1984, p. 74.
3. Statutes of the Republic of South Africa – Defence, *Armaments Development and Production Act No. 57 of 1968* with Amendment Acts through 1982.
4. *Armaments Development and Production Act*, pp. 167–68.
5. *Armaments Development and Production Act*, p. 169.
6. Statutes of the Republic of South Africa – Arms and Ammunition, *Simulated Armaments Transactions Prohibition Act, No. 2 of 1976.*

Chapter 6
1. *Defence*, September 1987, p. 551.
2. *National Defense*, 'South African Composite Armor,' July/August 1987, p. 16.
3. *Military Technology*, 'South Africa's Helicopter Programme,' July 1987, p. 49.
4. *Military Technology*, July 1987, p. 50.
5. This material was researched through on-site investigation by the author. There is no published material that covers the inner-workings of the Armscor library. Interviews, informal conversations with Armscor executives utilising the library, questioning of staff members and a systematic perusal of literature in the library were used in this research.

Chapter 7
1. *Sunday Tribune*: 'Danger of War with Red Giant', 15 November 1987.
2. *Sunday Star*: 'The Angola Dilemma: To Get More Involved or to Pull Out Now', 22 November 1987.
3. *Sunday Tribune*: 15 November 1987.
4. *Duncan Innes*: Writes and lectures on privatisation and deregulation in South

Africa. He is an associate professor in the Department of Sociology at the University of the Witwatersrand, Johannesburg.

5. *Defence*: 'South African Defence Budget up by Almost 30%', Helmoed-Römer Heitman, August 1987, p. 450.
6. *Defence*: p. 451.
7. *The Star*: Information garnered through intelligence sources and indicated in *Star*, 'France will help protect Cape Route' 11 January 1988.
8. *Jane's Defence Weekly*.
9. *Pretoria News*: 'S.A. "Can produce its own Stingers" ', 3 April 1986.
10. *Citizen*: 'Explosive Factory near city to Close', 26 September 1987.
11. *Armscor*: 'A Giant in South African Industry', no date, p. 18.
12. *South African Institute of International Affairs*: Seminar, Jan Smuts House, University of the Witwatersrand, 'South Africa's Neighbours', 19 November 1987.
13. *Star*: 'Blaring Sirens for S.A. Sanctions get a Shrug', Ken Vernon, 21 November 1987.
14. *Star*: 'Homeland Units part of SADF, body claims', 20 November 1987.

Review of Literature and Bibliography

Except for an historical treatise of arms manufacturing in South Africa since the Second World War, the overwhelming majority of literature post-dates 1960. It is important to note that the manufacturing of arms and munitions were not of critical importance to the South Africa Government until after the United Nations arms embargo of 1963. Therefore, the UN arms embargo of '63 and the mandatory arms embargo of '77 became central to this study.

A rather illuminating phenomenon is the historical treatment and rationale used by the Republic in telling the story of Armscor. It readily outlines the objective, arms boycott, history, Board of Directors, organisation, procurement procedure, role of the private sector, subsidiaries, production highlights, training, marketing and finance albeit superficially, but nevertheless with verve in its standard glossy public relations booklets. *This is Armscor* and *Armscor, A Giant in the South African Industry.*

Because the arms embargo and the implementation thereto, has taken on a central role in the South African question, it has become mandatory to examine one secondary source and two primary sources which chronologically treat the connection of the arms embargo and the arms procurement of South Africa from the early 1960s to the present, viz. the *New York Times*, US Congressional Hearings of the Committees of Foreign Affairs (House) and Relations (Senate); and United Nations documents, i.e. General Assembly sessions, Security Council Committees, Special Reports, Reports from the Department of Political and Security Council Affairs (Centre Against Apartheid). Various newspapers such as the *Washington Post, London Times, Daily*

Telegraph, Manchester Guardian, Financial Mail, Rand Daily Mail, Star, Cape Times, Post (Natal Edition and *Pretoria News*) are central to events that pertain to South Africa. They provide the news on places, events and people that can be further examined through the original sources. Nevertheless, the above resources are not exhaustive.

South African military magazines such as *Militaria, Uniform, Paratus* and *Armed Forces* give the status and operational usage data of military systems such as the new 'Hopper' radio manufactured by Grinaker Electronics and the Casspir combat vehicle. *Salvo*, an internal Armscor magazine contains a wealth of information. These can be cross checked by the latest *Military Balance* published by the International Institute of Strategic Studies. The *South African Digest* is reliable for limited extracts on military capabilities such as the following:

> A South African engineer has designed what is claimed to be the world's most advanced drone or pilotless aircraft. The craft, which is 3.78 m long can be used for both reconnaissance and attack purposes.... The craft, which has been dubbed the Eyrie, is believed to be more advanced than the American Skyeye.... The Eyrie will be marketed internationally. Six planes with spares will cost about R8-million.[1]

Jane's up-to-date series on aircraft, small arms, warships and weapons systems, *Jane's Defence Weekly*, along with *Navy International, International Defense Review, South African Defence Force, Defence and Foreign Affairs, National Defence, Military Technology, Defence, Armada International, Flight International, Air International, Interavia, Aeronautical Journal, Armor, Aviation Week and Space Technology, Defence Africa, Defense and Foreign Affairs Weekly, International Combat Arms, Maritime Defence International, Military Technology, Security Gazette,* and *Defense and Foreign Affairs Handbook,* provide the latest on weapons systems and munitions in addition to their capabilities. These periodicals are of importance because the reader is able to glean from these the capabilities of existing systems and to determine if these weapons capabilities are the existing technological state of the art within Armscor. If not, inferences can be drawn and additional follow-up may indicate a circumvention of the arms embargo and possibly a connection to the 'Fifth World' (Israel, Taiwan, South Korea, Chile and Argentina).

Policy determination and a wealth of information on defence (the threat), role of the services, manpower, logistics, budget and armaments supply are found in the *White Paper on Defence and Armaments Supply,*

1984–86, published by the Republic of South Africa, Department of Defence. The 1984 White Paper, emphasises the continuing arms build-up. The aims posited in the 1986 White Paper of Armscor and the SADF is to '… meet the anticipated demands and requirements of an effective armed force to counter the onslaught against the RSA.' A cursory look at selective weapons systems, failure of the arms embargo, direct sales, the computer connection, commercial sales and the licencing process is contained in the March 1986 *Bulletin of the Atomic Scientists*. In addition, numerous unpublished documents are available which provide new information or corroborate existing information. These include studies of theses, government memos/ publications, papers and notes. The Christian Concern for Southern Africa (CCSA) *Arms for Apartheid* and *Armscor and the South African Defence Industry* are but a few examples.

There are numerous books that sporadically cover the arms embargo, SADF and Armscor but no one volume that deals exclusively with the issue – *African Armies, Evolution and Capabilities, The Struggle for South Africa, Munger Africana Library Notes, Southern Africa: The Continuing Crisis, White Wealth and Black Poverty, The Political Economy of South Africa, South Africa, 1986, A Short Research Guide on Arms and Armed Forces, U.S. Arms Deliveries to South Africa, The Apartheid War Machine, U.S. Military Involvement in Southern Africa, Which Way is South Africa Going? Why South Africa will Survive, South Africa in Namibia, South African Politics, The Apartheid Regime, South Africa: Time Running Out, A U.S. Policy Toward South Africa, South Africa's War Machine, Pretoria's Praetorians* and *The Militarisation of South African Politics*. As such, an extensive bibliography can be forthcoming which tends to be large in volume but limited in substance on this particular issue.

Although not directly dealing with Armscor, *Foreign Policy*, a quarterly, *Business Week, Forbes*, the *Economist, Africa Review, Africa Confidential, South Africa Forum*, and the *South Africa International* provide a wealth of information on politico-military affairs as well as sanctions and the arms embargo.

Research was conducted on site in South Africa and in London, England. Because of the nature of the subject and the dearth of public information published by South Africa, it became necessary to conduct personal interviews within South Africa. Although not too tenuous, nevertheless this led to an interactive process whereby evidence already uncovered was linked, forming a mosaic which heretofore had not been uncovered.

An assessment of the literature indicated that reseach was necessary from numerous sources, plus on-site investigation and personal interviews. The latter proved to be rewarding. Ostensibly, the present situation in South Africa must be considered when dealing with this subject. 'The arms embargo requires Armscor to operate behind a legislatively enforced veil of secrecy and sometimes to use methods that might seem more appropriate to an intelligence service than an industrial undertaking.'[2]

Books

Adams, John, *The Unnatural Alliance*, London: Quartet Books, 1984.

Albrecht, U. *et al.*, *A Short Research Guide on Arms and Armed Forces*, London: Croom Helm, 1978.

Arlinghaus, B., and Baker, P., eds., *African Armies, Evolution and Capabilities*, Boulder, Col.: Westview Press, 1986.

A U.S. Policy Toward South Africa, 'The Report of the Secretary of State's Advisory Committee on South Africa', Department of State, 29 January 1987.

Carter, Gwendolen M., *Which Way is South Africa Going?* 1980.

Carter, Gwendolen M., and O'Meara, Patrick, eds., *Southern Africa: The Continuing Crisis*, Bloomington: Indiana University Press, 1982.

Carter, Gwendolen M., *Which Way is South Africa Going?* 1980.

Cawthra, Gavin, *Brutal Force, The Apartheid War Machine*, London: International Defence and Aid Fund, May 1986.

Davies, R., and O'Meara, D., *The Stuggle for South Africa*, London: Zed Press, 1985.

Defense and Foreign Affairs Handbook, Washington, D.C.: Perth, 1986.

Enloe, Cynthia, *Police, Military and Ethnicity: Foundations of State Power*, London: Transaction Books, 1980.

Foltz, W.J., and Beinen, H.S., *Arms and the African*, A Council on Foreign Relations Book, 1984.

Frankel, Phillip H., *Pretoria's Praetorians*, Cambridge: Cambridge University Press, 1984.

Gann, Lewis H., *Why South Africa Will Survive: A Historical Analysis*, New York: St. Martins, 1981.

Geldenhuys, Deon, *The Diplomacy of Isolation*, Johannesburg: Macmillan for the South African Institute of International Affairs, 1984.

Grundy, Kenneth W., *Soldiers Without Politics: Blacks in the South African Armed Forces*, Berkley: University of California Press, 1983.

Grundy, Kenneth W., *The Militarization of South African Politics*, London: I.B. Tauris & Co., Ltd., 1986.

Jaster, Robert S., *South Africa in Namibia: The Botha Strategy*, New York: Harvard, University Press of America, 1985.

Jaster, Robert S., 'South Africa Defense Strategy and the Growing Influence of the Military', in Williams J. Foltz and Henry S. Bienen, eds., *Arms and the African*, New Haven: York University Press, 1985.

Klare, M.T., *US Arms Deliveries to South Africa*, Washington, D.C.: Transnational Institute, 1977.

Lang, Kurt, *Military Institutions and the Sociology of War*, Beverly Hills: Sage, 1972.

Military Balance, London: International Institute for Strategic Studies, 1986.

Moorcraft, Paul L., *Africa's Superpower*, Johannesburg, Sygma Book/ Collins, 1981.

Omond, Roger, *The Apartheid Handbook: A Guide to South Africa's Everyday Racial Policies*, Harmondsworth: Penguin Books.

Price, Robert M., *The Apartheid Regime: Political Power and Racial Domination*, Berkley: Institute of International Studies, University of California.

South Africa: Time Running Out, The Report of the Study Commission on U.S. Policy Toward Southern Africa, University of California Press, Foreign Policy Study Foundation, Inc., 1981.

Stander, Siegfried, *Like the Wind*, Cape Town: Saagman and Weber, 1985.

Statutes of the Republic of South Africa – Defence – Arms and Ammunition, 'Armaments Development and Production Act No. 57 of 1968', amended, 'Simulated Armaments Transaction Prohibition Act No. 2 of 1976', and 'Defence Special Account Act No. 6 of 1974'.

Thompson, Leonard, *The Political Mythology of Apartheid*, New Haven, Yale University Press, 1985.

Thompson, Leonard, and Prior, Andrew, *South African Politics*, New Haven: Yale University Press, 1982.

Tylden, G., *The Armed Forces of South Africa*, Johannesburg: City of Johannesburg Africana Museum, Frank Connock Publications, No. 2, 1954.

U.S. Dept. of State, Bureau of Public Affairs, Office of Historian, The U.S. and S.A.: U.S. Public Statements and Related Documents, 1977–1985, Research Project No. 1467, Sept. 1985.

−Doc. No. 176 − Executive Order 12532 of 9 September, 1985.
−Doc. No. 12 − UNSCR 418 (1977) of 4 October 1977.
−Doc. No. 153 UNSCR 558 (1984) of 13 December 1984.

Walters, Ronald W., *South Africa and the Bomb: Responsibility and Deterrence*, Lexington, Mass: Lexington Books, 1987.
Western Massachusetts Association of Concerned African Scholars, *US Military Involvement in Southern Africa*, Boston: South End Press, 1978.

In addition, a substantial bibliography of articles from periodical journals and newspapers exists, too extensive for publication in this book.

Notes
1. 'Advanced SA-Designed Drone', *South African Digest*, 30 May 1986, p. 480.
2. 'Behind the Secrecy Shroud', *South African Digest*, 8 January 1982, p. 16.

Index